THINKING
OTHERWISE

A
Living Faith
Book

Living Faith books are for readers who cherish the life of the mind and the things of the Spirit. Each title offers an example of faith in search of understanding, the unique voice of a practicing scholar who has cultivated a believing heart.

OTHER LIVING FAITH BOOKS INCLUDE:

Samuel M. Brown, *First Principles and Ordinances: The Fourth Article of Faith in Light of the Temple*

George B. Handley, *The Hope of Nature*

George B. Handley, *If Truth Were a Child*

Ashley Mae Hoiland, *One Hundred Birds Taught Me to Fly: The Art of Seeking God*

Patrick Q. Mason, *Planted: Belief and Belonging in an Age of Doubt*

Adam S. Miller, *Letters to a Young Mormon* (2nd ed.)

Steven L. Peck, *Evolving Faith: Wanderings of a Mormon Biologist*

Thomas F. Rogers, *Let Your Hearts and Minds Expand: Reflections on Faith, Reason, Charity, and Beauty*

Melissa Wei-Tsing Inouye, *Crossings: A Bald Asian American Latter-day Saint Woman Scholar's Ventures through Life, Death, Cancer & Motherhood (Not Necessarily in That Order)*

THINKING OTHERWISE

THEOLOGICAL EXPLORATIONS OF

JOSEPH SMITH'S REVELATIONS

JAMES E. FAULCONER

BYU
Maxwell
Institute

Neal A. Maxwell Institute for Religious Scholarship
Brigham Young University, Provo, UT

Permissions. No portion of this book may be reproduced by any means or process without the formal written consent of the publisher. Direct all permissions requests to: Permissions Manager, Neal A. Maxwell Institute for Religious Scholarship, Brigham Young University, Provo, UT 84602.

The paper used in this publication meets the minimum requirements of the American National Standard for Information Sciences—Permanence of Paper for Printed Library Materials. ANSI Z39.48-19

ISBN: 978-1-9503-0400-4

Art Direction: Blair Hodges

Cover design: Heather Ward

Book design: Carmen Durland Cole

Printed in the United States of America

http://maxwellinstitute.byu.edu/

Library of Congress Cataloging-in-Publication Data
Names: Faulconer, James E., author.
Title: Thinking otherwise : theological explorations of Joseph Smith's revelations / James E Faulconer.
Description: Provo, UT : Neal A. Maxwell Institute for Religious Scholarship, Brigham Young University, [2020] | Series: Living faith | Includes index. | Summary: "Noting how the problematical framework of Western thinking came to dominate reflection on divine matters, Faulconer discusses some of Joseph Smith's teachings that contradict that tradition, focusing particularly on the teaching that God is embodied. Then he offers an alternative way of doing theology, namely performative theology, followed by examples"-- Provided by publisher.
Identifiers: LCCN 2020025937 | ISBN 9781950304004 (paperback)
Subjects: LCSH: Church of Jesus Christ of Latter-day Saints--Doctrines. | Mormon Church--Doctrines.
Classification: LCC BX8635.3 .F35 2020 | DDC 230/.93--dc23
LC record available at https://lccn.loc.gov/2020025937

DEDICATION

To Samuel, Charlotte, Hannah, Margaret, Madison, Brigham, Benjamin, Asa, Chase, Ellen, Clara, Davis, Penelope, Phoenix, . . .

Contents

Introduction

I f you have picked up and opened this book, one of two sce-
narios seems likely: either you are just curious about what
theology is, or you have an interest in Latter-day Saint theology. In the second case, perhaps you have read some of the
nineteenth-century Latter-day Saint theologians. Perhaps you
were one of those who sat up late at night in the university dor-
mitory, trying to figure out Anselm's proof of God's existence
after philosophy class. Or you may do theology in a book club, as
an occasion for getting together with friends as much as to talk
about theology.

Not everyone wants to do theology as undertaken in this
book: thoughtful reflection on the authoritative teachings of The
Church of Jesus Christ of Latter-day Saints—in other words, its
doctrines. Almost no one needs to. Even when one has good reason for doing it, there is no question that theological thinking
takes a back seat to *doing*. Trust in the Lord means doing things,
not only believing them or figuring out how one belief relates to
another. Trust in God means caring for the poor and oppressed

as one among them, bearing one another's burdens (see, e.g., Psalm 146:5–7; Isaiah 1:17; Mosiah 18:8–9; 3 Nephi 24:5). It means being baptized and keeping covenant with God and our fellows in the way we live our lives. We cannot claim either to trust God or to worship him if the practices of our religion are not central to our understanding of it.

As true as that is, there are nevertheless occasions when one needs to do theology. Sometimes the need is ethical: someone has asked me a question about the Church's teachings—perhaps a person of another faith, perhaps a struggling brother or sister—and I am obliged to respond with reasons for those teachings. Sometimes the need is psychological: I have the theological *dis*-ease, an itch that wants scratching, and theology is the only lidocaine available to stop me from scratching until I bleed. Other times the theological need may be merely a matter of pleasure: it's fun and enlightening to think with friends about questions of theology, to try one's answers out against the responses of others, as in the debates that Joseph Smith and other early Latter-day Saints organized in the lyceums and debating societies of Nauvoo. For some of us, there is yet another reason: doing the thinking required by theology helps deepen our faith. We start with faith, in other words trust, in what we have learned through the testimony of the Holy Ghost, and through theological reflection our faith is strengthened, made deeper.

This book is directed at Latter-day Saints who, for whatever reason, feel the need to do theology. Perhaps it will help you think differently about how to explain your religion to those who ask you about it. It's an offering to those who are struggling: perhaps thinking otherwise about your questions will help you. I hope it is additional balm for those with the theological itch, as well as added pleasure for those doing theology for the fun of it. More than that, I hope that the different kind of theology for which I will argue will in the end help some who read this deepen their faith.

The most important assumption driving this book is that we have seldom thought through Joseph Smith's teachings without quietly, usually unknowingly, importing large chunks of theology that are incongruent with his teachings. In particular, we have inherited a concept of God that conflicts with the nature of God as he is revealed through Joseph Smith (e.g., as embodied, sexed, and eternally among other beings). Those two ways of understanding the divine are profoundly different, and their differences should give us a very different understanding of things theological.

Yet, though we acknowledge and even celebrate that Joseph Smith reveals a different God and a different way of thinking about religion, we seldom follow through to the theological differences his revelations imply. What difference does belief that God is embodied make, for example, to how we understand what it means to say that he is perfect? Can we assume that traditional theological thought about what it means to be a perfect being is relevant to thinking about what perfection means for the God in whom we believe? The undergirding assumption of this book is that thinking as Joseph Smith's revelations teach us to think ought to make us think otherwise than the Western philosophical tradition. I doubt that our thinking will be orthogonal to that tradition. It's not clear how that would be possible. But it will be at least askew of it.

Thinking differently about Joseph Smith's teachings will require that we first are able to see how they contrast with teachings of the Western Christian tradition. To make that contrast, chapter 1 gives a brief historical overview of how, for the most part, the Christian tradition came to understand God as it does, and chapter 2 explores what this means for theology. Against that background, chapter 3 takes a stab at showing some of the import of Joseph Smith's teachings. I try to think about how latter-day revelation offers an alternative to the tradition as I sketch out a few of the many theological consequences of taking Joseph Smith's teachings seriously.

The first thing to recognize when doing any theology, though, is that one's thinking can only be provisional. To explain is to say, "In the present circumstances, this is what I would say." The circumstances can vary according to time, place, and audience. My knowledge changes. The audience changes. The relationships important to one instance are different from those important to another. The experiences relevant to my thinking are different this time from what they were another time. These sorts of differences mean that my theological explanations will also vary. As some thoughtful friends have said, "Latter-day Saint theology is always local." Those differences between my thinking about my faith and the thinking of someone else, or between my thinking at one time and another, ought not to worry me. To give up on final answers isn't to give up on everything. There can be good answers and answers that are good enough for our purposes even if there is no final answer. There is a God to whom we are related, and he reveals himself and his answers to us through the prophets.

Our *relationship* to God and to others whom we love and respect is a firm base on which we can stand. The consequence of having that base is that we are related to one another and to the world differently than we would be otherwise. But it doesn't follow that when we step back and reflect on what those relations and revelations mean, we will eventually come to a final answer, at least not in this life. Absolute relations don't imply absolute answers.

I believe there is no one answer to "What does all this mean?"—perhaps not even in the eternities—because the real world is thick enough, rich enough, that no one answer will ever do. Those who believe in a metaphysical being of some kind that is outside space and time and that overarches and gives unity to all that is could, perhaps, believe that there is such an ultimate answer, one that ends all need to speak and discuss. But if there is no such being, and I believe Joseph Smith's teachings imply there is not, then there is no reason to believe there is ultimately only one answer to our questions—nor is there any need to believe that the only alternative is some kind of absolute relativism.

So I will try to suggest some ways in which Joseph Smith taught things that ought to make us think quite differently about theological questions. Nevertheless, as important as I believe that is, my discussion of Latter-day Saint doctrinal theology and the implications of Joseph Smith's revelations about God is not my primary interest. This leads me to the second assumption driving this book.

Though I recognize the place of doctrinal theology, I believe another way of doing theology is less likely, rather than unlikely, to be influenced by concepts inherited from the Christian tradition. That other way of doing theology comes from asking whether the twin sisters of philosophy and doctrinal theology are the best ways for talking about God and the things of God. Is there another, perhaps even better, way to "stretch as high as the utmost heavens, and search into and contemplate the darkest abyss, and expanse of eternity," as Joseph Smith urged the Saints to do?[1]

I argue that there is: theology can also be done by thoughtful analysis of and response to the word of God in scripture: scripture study. Though scripture study doesn't produce the kinds of more or less final answers to abstract questions that dogmatic

---

1. Joseph Smith, "History, 1838–1856, volume C-1 [2 November 1838–31 July 1842]," p. 904b, The Joseph Smith Papers, https://www.josephsmithpapers .org/paper-summary/history-1838-1856-volume-c-1-2-november-1838 -31-july-1842/86.

theology does, it is an alternative to dogmatic theology. It may sometimes be an even better way to do theology than creating logically coherent sets of propositions that describe one's beliefs and how they relate to one another. As scripture study, theology takes the word *theology* (*theos*, or "God," plus *logos*, or "language") to mean "what God says to us" rather than "what we say about him."

Understood in that sense, theology isn't *based in* scripture study, it *is* scripture study. It is scripture study because scripture is a revelation of the truth of our relation to God. Because theology in this sense reveals the truth of the living Christ and our living relationship with him, it is not merely a list of static, unchanging propositions about him. It is an account of the experience of the invitation to come into relationship with God. It is an account of the experience of the love of God: he shows himself to us if we are willing to receive him, but he will not impose himself on us. (That is one reason that knowledge of God cannot be a matter of certainty.) If I claim to be doing theology, then I claim to be trying to show others how scripture shows God's love. If I am successful, presumably what I say will be an invitation to my readers to the same experience. In contrast to dogmatic theology, I will describe a way of reading scripture closely called "performative theology," in which the point of close reading is to show us that scripture calls us to Christ and how that is done.

The result of my two assumptions—that we do not usually take seriously enough the theological implications of Joseph Smith's revelations and that performative theology is an alternative to dogmatic theology—is that this book has six chapters. The first is a discussion of the Eternal One and some instances where it shows up in philosophy and theology. Second is a chapter that addresses the question of what I think this inherited notion means for Latter-day Saints doing theology. That is followed by a chapter with a few thoughts about how Joseph Smith's teachings differ from that of the Eternal One and the implications of his teachings for thinking about God. The fourth chapter discusses how scripture study can be an alternative to other kinds of theology, an alternative called performative theology. The fifth chapter begins with a discussion of how to do the close reading of performative theology; this is followed by an example, a reading of Moses 5. The sixth and final chapter is another illustration, an analysis of Doctrine and Covenants 121.

Neither of the two interpretations of scripture in the last two chapters is intended to be definitive. Instead, each intends to show us one way of reading the verses in question. Other readers who see different details in the text on different occasions with different questions in mind as they read will give different readings of the scriptures I've chosen to write about. And, presumably, that could be done over and over again.

Before going forward, let me express my gratitude. I am indebted to many who made this book possible, but I can mention only a few in particular: the Wheatley Institution and the Neal A. Maxwell Institute for Religious Scholarship, both at Brigham Young University, who gave me the time needed for thinking and writing; Logan Packer, who did much of the legwork required; Miranda Wilcox and Morgan Davis, whose responses clarified and improved my thinking and writing; and Don Brugger, whose suggestions made this book make more sense than it would have otherwise. Thanks to you and to the many friends and assistants who have helped me at various stages of this book's progress.

CHAPTER ONE

The One and the Many

Very few people today are kept up at night by the philosophical problem of the One and the Many: Is what-is, taken as a totality, ultimately just one thing, or is it multiplicity all the way down? Can we ultimately explain the universe and all that is in terms of only one thing, whether that is God or a particular subatomic particle? Or is any explanation we give always going to require us to refer to more than one thing—namely, God plus something else, such as multiple kinds of particles? If we opt for the former, then we assume "the One." If we opt for the latter, then we are putting our money on "the Many." Or, as many thinkers have argued, is the problem that for a very long time we have been thinking about what it means to be in the wrong terms?[1] The problem is abstruse, to be

---

1. Many have argued that to be a thing is to have effects in the world rather than to be a substance: substances (e.g., rocks) have effects, but not all things that have effects (e.g., French verbs) are substances. If this is right, then the question about whether there is one substance or many substances is misguided. I fall into the camp of those who think the question is misguided, but since it is a question that has directed philosophical and theological thinking for several thousand years, I will use it as a heuristic device.

sure. You might talk about it in a beginning philosophy class, though I also wouldn't be surprised if you did not. Yet, in spite of its seeming irrelevance to most of us most of the time, that question—whether what-is is fundamentally one or many—and philosophy's answer to it is at the heart of Christian theology. (Given what is at the heart of theology, perhaps the best thing to do would be to drive a stake through it, but even then it would be too late.)

The question of the One or the Many has its beginnings in the philosophical discussions of antiquity, at least six hundred years before Christ. The issue shows up at various points in the history of Western thought over more than two millennia, and seeing how it does will help us more easily see how Joseph Smith's teaching is different. I cannot do that, however, without scandalously oversimplifying the thinkers I will be talking about. A reader might think of the things I say about individuals or movements as bullet points in a slide presentation. They will certainly not be a careful exposition.[2]

Alternatively, think of travelers in a strange country. Travelers sometimes need to ask where they are. Perhaps they are lost. Perhaps they are not lost but are not completely confident in their surroundings. Or perhaps they are *too* confident in their ability to answer that question, confident but mistaken nonetheless. They have lost their bearings, and getting them requires an answer to the question, Where are we in relation to other places? Hikers might get an answer by finding a high spot from which to get a look at the geography. Drivers might answer the question by consulting an electronic map, which gives them an even higher spot—a view that is ultimately from a satellite—from which to take a look at their surroundings. For us, too, that high spot won't give us the details of what we are looking at. We will

---

2. I will, though, provide suggested readings for further study in the appendix.

miss a great deal. None of us seeing Seoul or Paris with a satellite's view will have a good sense of the reality of either city. We certainly wouldn't consider ourselves to be sightseers, much less inhabitants. But sometimes the overlook will allow us to make general points that help us compare things. A view from above might allow us to see, for example, that in spite of their differences, Seoul and Paris are each bisected by the arc of a great river, and that might lead us to ask questions about them that we might otherwise not think of.

Similarly, we need an overview from which to think about both traditional Western Christianity and the restoration that began with Joseph Smith so we can see what our thinking may have relied on unconsciously, as well as consciously, and what it *can* rely on. Our overview cannot take in everything, but we can take in some general points here and there that will help us better understand how the position where we find ourselves in the Restoration is different from other, related positions.

ORIGINS OF THE PROBLEM

The problem of the One and the Many may well seem like an abstruse philosophical conundrum with little relation to anything. But bear with me for a moment. An overview will, I believe, show that it is more implicate in our thinking than we might imagine. In spite of the apparently arcane nature of the problem, and though few know the name Parmenides (pronounced Par-mén-uh-deez), perhaps no one has had more influence on how we think and talk about God in the West than he has, though he lived twenty-five hundred years ago in the Greek colony of Elea (Velia in modern Italy). Western thought and those influenced by it have tiptoed around his views. They have often ignored, not worried about, or not known that he is the original source of the concepts that structure much of their philosophical and theological thinking. In spite of that, in the West anyone talking about God after Parmenides has done so using some version of the terms he set out in discussing the problem of the One and the Many.

Like other early Greek philosophers, Parmenides was concerned with how to explain change in the world. We live in a world of changing appearances. The acorn becomes an oak. The wind moves the leaves of the trees. The seasons bring new growth and then the dieback of fall and the hibernation of winter. Thinkers before Parmenides had explained those changes with talk about gods like Zeus, Hera, and Herakles. To some degree, the earliest philosophers agreed with those mythological thinkers: there is more to this world than what we see, and whatever that more-than is explains the change we experience. But for the first philosophers, the notion of notoriously changeable gods was not a satisfactory answer to their question, What explains change? Instead, they looked for what is unchanging, something that remains the same throughout all change. To explain the instability of change that they saw all around them, they wanted something stable and common to everything. For the most part, they also wanted *one* thing to explain everything rather than a multiplicity. Their assumption that change needs to be explained by something unchanging and that ultimately it could have only one explanation became determinative for the next several thousand years of thinking about the world.

Ancient Greek thinkers suggested a variety of substances that could perhaps be that one thing common to all things at every time: water, air, fire, mind. But Parmenides took a giant philosophical step when he said that whatever was ultimate couldn't be any of those things or any other element of this world. He agreed with most of the other early philosophers that, ultimately, there can be only one thing that accounts for everything else. He called his explanation of what is ultimate "The Way of Truth."

What truly is, he argued, is absolutely one and indivisible, without parts. Not only that, he argued, whatever the ultimate thing is, it must be omnipresent (present everywhere at the same time). So, in distinction from what "The Way of Opinion"—in other words, the way of our senses and everyday experience—teaches us, Parmenides concluded that what truly is must be unchangeable and must be something other than or beyond the world that we experience. That is the Way of Truth.

Parmenides's answer to the question of change was that behind the appearances we experience, like an invisible but permanent and stable framework that supports the world of experience, there must be some reality that is unchanging, something *more* real than what we experience. Our senses show us a world of change and multiplicity, but—supposedly—reason shows that world to be unreal and reveals the unseen and unchanging, ultimately real world that is somehow responsible for the world of change.

We could diagram Parmenides's view like this:

WHAT IS ULTIMATE; WHAT IS REAL

WHAT WE EXPERIENCE; WHAT IS LESS REAL,
MADE POSSIBLE BY WHAT IS ULTIMATE

Parmenides's view of reality.

In the end, anything we experience can be explained only by referring to what transcends our world, a "metaphysical world" in philosophy-speak. (*Metaphysical* literally means "beyond the physical.") As he is usually interpreted, Parmenides gave careful rational arguments that the transcendent ultimate must not only be unchanging, it must be unmoving, indivisible, unaffected, and outside time—since each of those implies change. Having made his argument for the nature of ultimate reality, Parmenides unknowingly set the parameters for most future talk about God in the West: believers took deity to be the one ultimate thing, outside space and time, that does not change in any way and that accounts for everything that is.

It is important to remember that Parmenides himself wasn't thinking about anything like what Jews and Christians think of when they speak of God. Parmenides called the ultimate thing "the One." It was not a divine person, and that was crucial to Parmenides's point: what is ultimate is not personal. It is not like the traditional Greek gods. Later Greek thinkers, such as Aristotle (384–322 BC), used the word *god* (*theos* in Greek, from which we get the word *theology*) for their versions of Parmenides's One, but neither did they have in mind anything like the personal God of the Hebrew Bible, the New Testament, or latter-day scripture. That is the first clue that there may be a problem of fit between the two sets of ideas.

> Parmenides argues that what is ultimately real must be unchanging, and thereby he gives Western culture its ways of thinking about God: an Eternal One.

Plato (428/427–348/347 BC) wrote a careful criticism of Parmenides's ideas in his dialogue titled *Parmenides*.[3] He argued that if the One has the kind of transcendence that Parmenides attributed to it, then we can say nothing about it because it is completely inaccessible to our minds. Or if, instead, it is the unity of the world we experience, then if we speak at all we are talking about it. So if there is a One, then either we cannot say

---

3. Plato, *Parmenides*, trans. Mary Louise Gill and Paul Ryan (Indianapolis, IN: Hackett, 1996).

anything about it or it doesn't matter what we say. Plato's implication is that the One is an unreasonable idea.

EARLY CHRISTIAN THINKING

In spite of Plato's argument, it was difficult to escape the pull of Parmenides's thinking. Even Plato found it difficult, in spite of himself, and several hundred years later Greco-Roman intellectual culture of the first century of Christianity inherited a Parmenidean notion of God: whatever is truly ultimate must be a version of the One; whatever is ultimately real cannot be the Many, ultimately multiple and irreducible to one thing. For Roman and early Christian thinkers, the idea came through Plato and Aristotle, but mostly their later understanding of Plato, and especially the understanding of Plato we find in Philo, a Jewish contemporary of Paul.[4] Plato and Aristotle were responding to Parmenides, though, and in different ways; and without completely acknowledging it, they accepted his understanding of what whatever is ultimate must be like. So when later thinkers began to think about the Jewish and Christian God philosophically—as they had to from at least the second century on—they tended to do so in Parmenides's terms. Those were, after all, the intellectual common currency of the time, the ideas available to early Christian thinkers for explaining their beliefs to others. They could have no more thought in other terms than we could explain how our houses are lit without using the language of electricity.

Those trying to think about God in Christianity shared the Parmenidean notion (though unconsciously) because they, too,

---

4. For an excellent discussion of many of these questions, see Christoph Markschies, *God's Body: Jewish, Christian, and Pagan Images of God*, trans. Alexander Johannes Edmonds (Waco, TX: Baylor University Press, 2019), e.g., 5–36.

were Greco-Romans. Even many centuries after Parmenides, Christian thinkers tended to think of God as in some way like Parmenides's One. Parmenides hadn't been thinking about what Christians meant by the word *God*, because he lived five hundred years before Christ. Nevertheless, Parmenides had laid out categories for understanding the nature of reality in terms of the metaphysical One and the physical Many that dominated Greco-Roman thought for many centuries. Parmenides's way of thinking about reality became an embedded cultural assumption. In fact, the Parmenidean assumption was all the more powerful because it was unconscious. Not knowing they were making that assumption made it difficult for early Christians to avoid it.

As you can imagine, for Christianity the Parmenidean implicit assumption was problematic even though it was invisibly constitutive of thinking about ultimate things for millennia. After all, it is not easy to integrate the Greek One with the notion of a Christian God, namely a heavenly Father, and his divine-human Son, Jesus Christ, who interact with us.[5] The One was unembodied, but Jesus had a body. The One was outside time, but Jesus was born, lived, and died in time. Christianity is a continuing response to that historical event, Jesus's life and death as a human person and his resurrection as a divine one. The One wasn't affected by the things of this world, but the Father hears prayers and Jesus felt joy, sorrow, and wonder. The One was impersonal, but each member of the Godhead is a person.

---

5. As we will see, in the Latter-day Saint tradition, the notion that "God" means "Heavenly Father" is doubly complicated: first by the fact that the Father and the Son are not one being, though both are God; second, by the fact that Latter-day Saints believe in a Heavenly Mother, who is also divine. I will discuss both of those issues in chapter 3, "A Few Doctrinal Claims: The Many without Anarchy." In the meantime, however, I will use the language that has been most common in both the traditional Christian and the Latter-day Saint traditions, referring to God as our Father unless specifically referring to the Son.

In fact, the One was not just impassible (not able to be affected by other beings), it was *beyond* being either passible or impassible. It wasn't just invisible, it was beyond either visibility or invisibility. It wasn't just immaterial, it was beyond categories like materiality and immateriality. And so on.

THE COUNCIL OF NICAEA: JESUS'S DIVINITY *AND* HUMANITY

Thinking about Christian belief in terms of the One was not easy. In spite of that, when non-Christians asked reasonable questions about Christianity or made unreasonable accusations, though it happened gradually, by the end of the third century Christians thinkers felt that the only conceptual materials for responding were those of Greek philosophy. An earlier option was to merely bear witness to the truth of the gospel and hope that this spiritual witness would carry the day. That is what seems to be behind the four Gospels of the New Testament. Latter-day Saint missionaries today still use that option, bearing testimony rather than making a logical case. That is a perfectly reasonable way to tell someone of a truth one holds. But sometimes something more than witness was needed. In that case, the early Christians' only alternative was to respond in terms of the One. They gave the best account of their faith they could in the terms available to them.

> For the first Christians, the language of Greek and Roman thought and culture was the only language available to explain their beliefs and practices to others.

One obvious solution to the seeming logical difficulty of understanding how Jesus could be both divine and human was to deny that Jesus was divine. This was the kind of solution demanded if one held the unconscious Parmenidean prejudice that to be the ultimate being is to be the One. So some argued that God worked through a man named Jesus but that he was otherwise an ordinary mortal. Another solution was to deny that Jesus was ever actually a human being; he *seemed* like one but wasn't really. He was a kind of apparition through which God worked. That, too, was a solution made in response to the hidden notion that whatever is ultimate must be like Parmenides's One. The problem of whether Jesus was both divine and human at the same time was a knotty one, and remained so for the first several hundred years of Christianity. It was the problem that made the Council of Nicaea necessary in AD 325.

> The Council of Nicaea was formed to settle arguments about how Jesus could be both divine and human, and in the process argued for what came to be the traditional understanding of the Trinity.

When Latter-day Saints have thought about the Council of Nicaea, they have done so mostly in terms of how the council tried to accommodate the Christian belief in the Father, the Son, and the Holy Ghost with the Parmenidean doctrine that whatever is ultimate must be single.[6] That is probably because of our doctrinal interest in thinking about the difference between the traditional view of God and our own. There is a point to our interest in what happened at Nicaea, where the bishops agreed on the doctrine of the Trinity: there is

---

6. For example, see Roberts's treatment in B. H. Roberts, *Falling Away* (Salt Lake City: Deseret Book, 1931), 47–48.

a One, namely God, who has three persons by which he makes himself known to us. Clearly that is very different from what Joseph Smith taught about God. Nevertheless, in many ways the philosophical arguments about the relationships among persons of the Trinity were a sideshow to the question of whether Jesus was both fully human and fully divine.

Those at Nicaea were wrestling with the question of how a divine being, a being who is in many respects understood to be like Parmenides's One, could make himself known in the world at all, much less as a human being. They were trying to find a way to use the concepts they knew, those ultimately inherited from Parmenides (a name that stands here for a concept or way of thinking more than the historical individual), to understand the things of the holy writings they used as a source of wisdom, the Bible. The bishops meeting at Nicaea wrestled with the question, How can what is outside time and space and all that it entails (in other words, the One) come into time and space? One result of their discussions was the conclusion that the Father and the Son must be one in substance because whatever is ultimate cannot be multiple. There cannot be two (or more) coexistent ultimate things.

In spite of their conclusion that the Father and Son must be one in substance, the Christians meeting in Nicaea were unwilling to give up the belief that Jesus was a real human being who was born, lived, and died, just as any other human being. And they were equally unwilling to give up the belief that he was a divine being, the Son of God and the divine Messiah who had come to rescue his people from sin and death through his resurrection. They genuinely believed both, and they set out to write a definition of their faith that would establish that they did, however difficult that might be philosophically. They believed that Jesus was fully human and fully divine, and they weren't going to give up the conjunction of those beliefs merely because it is difficult to explain philosophically how that is true. Those at Nicaea couldn't escape the tension between Christ's humanity and their understanding of his divinity, and they didn't try to. (And perhaps we should be uncertain that we understand what it means to say that Jesus was both divine and human—not because what we have been taught is untrue, but because we may not understand it.)

Christian thinkers have been wrestling with the conundrum of Jesus's humanity and divinity for almost two thousand years. During the last two hundred years or so, some have updated one or another of the solutions proposed in late antiquity. Perhaps the most common updated conclusion has been that Jesus wasn't divine, though God worked through him. It isn't difficult to find Christians who understand who Jesus was in those terms.[7] But many other Christians, probably most, have continued to insist on the traditional view that Jesus was both divine and human. Nevertheless, regardless of the position Christians take about Jesus's divinity, for all engaged in it the discussion continues to be structured by the Parmenidean understanding and its logic. Usually, though, it is structured that way unwittingly by the assumption that whatever is ultimate must be singular and outside time and space.

---

7. For example, the young Martin Luther King Jr. opted for that solution as a student. See Martin Luther King Jr., "The Humanity and Divinity of Jesus," https://kinginstitute.stanford.edu/king-papers/documents/humanity -and-divinity-jesus. David Brown suggests that the Dutch theologian Edward Schillebeeckx held this position. See Brown, *The Divine Trinity* (London: Duckworth Publishing, 1985), 138–42. And the liberation theologian Jon Sobrino, SJ, seems to have veered close to affirming the same belief. See "Notification on the Works of Father Jon Sobrino, SJ," http://www .vatican.va/roman_curia/congregations/cfaith/documents/rc_con_cfaith _doc_20061126_notification-sobrino_en.html. This heresy is tempting for contemporary theologians.

PARMENIDEAN THEOLOGICAL CONSEQUENCES

Jesus's incarnation wasn't the only problem faced by Christian thinkers. Most of the theological questions of the sixteen or seventeen hundred years following the Nicaean Council have been heavily indebted to Parmenides (though he is rarely if ever mentioned in the discussions). One result of this influence was the idea that the creation of the world must be "from nothing" because ultimately there can be nothing besides Parmenides's One, not even chaotic matter.

Plato and Aristotle didn't believe that. For them, matter was uncreated and equally as eternal as whatever is ultimate. Nor did Christians teach creation from nothing until the second century AD or later. But from at least the third century most Christian thinkers accepted the Parmenidean logic that if God is ultimate, then there is nothing before him and nothing in addition to him—except what he creates. That means that either he creates whatever exists besides himself from nothing or he creates it from himself. After all, there's nothing outside his existence to create it from.

> The logic of the Parmenidean One gives us the idea that the creation of the cosmos had to be from nothing by a Being outside of which there is nothing else.

Another theological consequence was the view that God cannot have a body because a Parmenidean One cannot[8]—he

---

8. Michel René Barnes argues, as I and others do, that we cannot deduce from biblical scripture that God does not have a body. Instead, Barnes says the belief that he does not have a body is a consequence of assuming that God

creates all bodies, so he doesn't have one himself, except as he takes one up for his own purposes, as he did in Jesus.

As I said in the beginning, I'm scandalously oversimplifying more than twenty-five hundred years of Western thought about God. I've left a great deal out that will make any good historian of theology grit his teeth in pain. Though I've mentioned Jesus's incarnation, my abbreviated discussion doesn't sufficiently emphasize that it has been a crucial conversation among Christian theologians. And the twists and turns and intricacies of the history of philosophy behind the moment in time I'm outlining have been much more complicated (and interesting) than I've portrayed them. Likewise, the actual thinkers (Parmenides, Plato, Aristotle, and so on) are much more interesting than I make them appear. I use those thinkers as points of focus for certain ideas in my history more than as the thinkers themselves. There are lots of variations and alternatives in the history of thought.

In spite of that, I think my portrayal gives an accurate skeletal outline of how the concepts we first encounter in ancient Greek thought of 500 BC have laid the ground for much of our thinking about God. In the West, thinking about God has meant thinking about something metaphysically ultimate; in turn, that has meant thinking about something that is beyond the world we inhabit, something like Parmenides's One.

MODERNISM AND THINKING ABOUT GOD

For my purposes, the next place to see how the One is implicit in our thinking is what philosophers call the modern period, from

---

must be "simple"; in other words, he must be like the Parmenidean One, without parts. See Barnes, "'Shining in the Light of Your Glory': Finding the Simple Reading of Scripture," *Modern Theology* 35, no. 3 (July 2019): 418–27.

the sixteenth century through the twentieth. This was a period of rapid and important change in Europe. Old verities, from religion to explanations of the natural world, came into question, and alternatives to the old verities arose. The early part of the modern era saw the development of perspectival painting, Protestantism and its variety of denominations, Copernican and Galilean astronomy, the invention of calculus, and the development of Newtonian physics, to name a few such developments.

One of the most significant changes of the time was the development of modern science. Drawing on developments in medieval thought in the fourteenth century, modern thinkers divided thinking into that which dealt with divine things (theology) and that which dealt with nature (science). Previously there had been no such division; all were part of the same whole.

The division was originally intended to protect the teachings of the Christian church. Some late medieval thinkers, such as William of Ockham and his conversation partners in the thirteenth century, believed that only those with scholarly training in understanding the Christian revelation ought to deal with questions of Christian belief. They argued that since human wisdom cannot understand divine things by itself, it should limit its research to the human world: science is about worldly things, things subject to time, things that change and progress, but theology has to do with things that do not change (in other words, ultimately, the One); so science should not assume that it has anything to say about theology. Thus, scholars like Ockham concluded that those without training in theology should stick to what they understand, such as the things of nature.[9]

But in the long run that attempt to keep theology pure from the speculations of nontheologians made religion irrelevant

---

9. See Louis Dupré, "The Fateful Separation," in *Passage to Modernity: An Essay in the Hermeneutics of Nature and Culture* (New Haven: Yale University Press, 1993), 167–89.

to the sciences. It provided the ground for secularizing them: the argument that worked for keeping science out of theology worked equally well for keeping theology out of science. Ockham had said that science ought not to presume to say anything about theology. The modernist mantra became that theology should not presume to say anything about science.

Taking the approach to scientific questions first advocated by those defending theology—namely, leaving God and godly things out of the discussion—is sometimes called "methodological atheism." However, because one need not assume an atheistic position to take a scientific approach, "methodological materialism" is probably a better term. As Steven Peck has pointed out, we don't expect the mechanic fixing a car to have any particular belief about God (though, for her own sake, we hope she is a believer).[10] But we do expect her to assume that the standard laws of the material universe apply in her work. She should assume there are no spiritual powers involved in causing the car's problems, and she should use what she knows about material causation to solve those problems. Methodological materialism doesn't require that a scientist—or a mechanic—be an atheist, only that she assume that, for the purposes of her work, the only things that concern her are the relationships that obtain in matter that is in motion.

This methodological result of the medieval distinction between theology and the other ways of knowing, namely methodological materialism, has had huge implications for science and, indeed, the rest of our thinking for seven hundred years. At times (but not always) it has turned against the religious context from which it was born. In any case, it has been at the heart of the

---

10. See Steven L. Peck, *Science: The Key to Theology*, vol. 1, *Preliminaries* (Salt Lake City: Common Consent, 2017), 76–77.

modern project. Without methodological materialism, science would not be what it is today.

The other thing necessary to modern science was the closely related notion of objectivity, the idea that knowledge requires us to remain neutral, unattached, and disinterested in what we claim to know. We may have an interest in the object of our study, of course, but if we want to have knowledge, we must set any partiality aside.

These two ideas, methodological materialism and objectivity, were crucial to the development of modern science. Without them modern science and technology and the benefits they have brought to human beings would have been impossible. Millions of human beings would have died early deaths or lived more difficult lives.

SCIENTISM RATHER THAN SCIENCE

But as noteworthy as the achievements of modern science have been, they had a price. Methodological materialism and objectivity—as crucial as they are to the foundation of science—became more than a methodology. In Western culture they came to be the very definition of not only knowledge in natural science, but *any* kind of knowledge at all, and as they did so, they cut us off from our world and each other and from God. What we now call "scientism" arose, the view that the knowledge proper to natural science is the model for knowledge in every area of life: all real knowledge is like the knowledge of natural science.

> The separation of theology from natural science made "methodological materialism" possible, which was necessary to the development of modern science.

The price we paid (which wasn't the only possible price) has been too high. As N. T. Wright reminds us in his 2018 Gifford Lectures, the one condition put on Goethe's Faust was that in order to have power and wealth, he must never love what he enjoys.[11] Objectivity requires detachment, but detachment makes love impossible. Like Faust, we are condemned, alienated from the most important things we want to know—the objects of our love, like God, other people, and even ourselves, things we cannot know if all true knowledge must be objective.

LOVE AND KNOWLEDGE

By making all knowledge objective, we have lost what thinkers had insisted on for almost two thousand years, from Plato through the High Middle Ages. For them, it was impossible to know the most important things without love. Medieval thinkers would never have thought that knowledge of God could be objective. (The word *objective*, after all, literally means "pertaining to objects," and neither God nor other people are objects.) Loving him and knowing him were, they would have said, inseparable. I know the members of my family differently than their friends know them because I love them differently. And it makes a good deal of sense to say that a person cannot really know one of my family members without loving them in some way. Ancient and medieval thinkers (as we see in Augustine and those influenced by him) insisted that knowledge based on love was fundamental to all other kinds, that it was the most important kind of knowledge and made other kinds possible.

To say that love is fundamental to knowledge is not to say that one must have a certain emotional affect to have knowledge.

---

11. Wright's lectures are as yet unpublished, but they are available as YouTube videos. His remark about Faust comes from the first lecture, https://www.youtube.com/watch?v=zdUM0ZB5zT0&feature.

Medieval thinkers did not understand love in merely affective terms; they and ancient thinkers believed that love itself has an epistemological dimension. One understanding was that while all have the faculty of love, that faculty must be initiated or educated in order for the loving person to understand. Education came in the same ways we use today: demonstration, witness, explanation, lecture, investigation, personal experience, and so on. The point of education wasn't to give one a degree of epistemological certainty, but to teach one what are the proper objects of love and what are the proper relationships of love. One of the ways of loving what-is was an accurate acquaintance with objects, in other words objective knowledge. But that was not the measure of all knowledge, just one of the ways of knowing.

So some thinkers offered what look to us like proofs for God's existence. They called them that and, consequently, accidentally led us to think they were giving quasi-scientific proofs. But for them *proof* meant "witness" as much as or more than "objective demonstration" because they didn't have the scientistic understanding of proof that we now have. The medieval understanding of proofs for God is related to our use of *proof* in cases where we mean something like "test." An artist's proof of an engraving is an impression of the engraving made to see whether it works. Understanding proofs of God's existence in that way, the person who offers them says something like, "This explanation will show that belief in God's existence is strong." Their proofs were not given as objective proofs that ought to convince a rational person, regardless of their relationship with God. They were given to fellow believers—fellow lovers—to help them understand better what they already believed because of their love for God. Their proofs for God's existence were to educate lovers of God, not to convince unbelievers.

In contrast, modern thinkers like René Descartes begin by sincerely offering proofs of God's existence, but in a new sense, our sense of proof as logical or objective demonstration. They offer them as convincing arguments (as opposed to clarifying and reinforcing explanations). It isn't long, though, until philosophers come to realize that there can be no objective proofs of divine existence in this new sense of "proof" any more than there can be objective proofs of a beloved one's love. Once modernism arrives, the only quasi-convincing reason modern thinkers offer to believe in God is that he is necessary to morality. In Dostoevsky's *The Brothers Karamazov*, Dmitri sums up the modern understanding when he tells Alyosha that without God everything is permitted.[12] In other words, he says that if we believe there is morality, then we must believe in God as its origin.

At first glance, modernism would appear to be a rejection of Parmenides's One. After all, it divided the things of God from the things of nature, and only the first of those two would seem to be connected to the One. But modernism was not the rejection of the One that it seemed to be. For one thing, most early modern scientists, Newton (1642–1726) for example, continued to believe in the traditional God even if they practiced methodological materialism in their science. Their investigations might be multiple, but the world itself could ultimately be explained by the One called "God."

For another thing, and more importantly, early modern scientists continued to assume that some one thing, at least the laws of nature taken as a whole, was a consistent, unchanging One that explained their investigations. The One didn't go away with the arrival of modernism. It merely took on a new form. Nevertheless, the loss of the One had begun, even if only implicitly and even though no one really noticed for quite some time.

---

12. Fyodor Dostoevsky, "A Hymn and a Secret," in *The Brothers Karamazov* (1880), part 4, book 11, chapter 4.

SCIENCE VERSUS RELIGION

By the eighteenth century, the division between science and religion became the antipathy that we recognize today, an antipathy in which science invariably has the upper hand. For people in the twenty-first century, the sciences have turned the tables on premodern thought: now all true knowledge is the knowledge of science (scientism—which is not the same as science); those who claim knowledge concerning divine things should adopt science as their way of knowing divine things—or, if not, they should stick to what they claim to know (supposedly only subjectively) and leave everything else to science.

> If knowledge doesn't presuppose love, the only proof of God's existence is that without him—without the One—there is no morality.

With science's rise to cultural power in the West, genuine atheism (a version of methodological materialism) became possible for the first time in a long time. Some reasoned that since science is the model for *all* knowledge and science gives no scientific reason for believing in God, it makes sense to assume there is no God.

However, even having separated the things of nature from the things of God, ironically, most scientists continued to believe in a One of some sort: pure reason, for example, or the ultimate system of knowledge that incorporates all understanding. Given that belief, many of them dreamed of one account of everything, a total scientific view of what makes the world what it is. But that dream was impossible because of the division of science from theology and especially the divisions within science itself—such as the differences between the various sciences, each different from the other, depending on what objects it investigates and how it investigates them. While the belief in the One continued in both religion and science, it was nevertheless beginning to unravel in science, as it had already unraveled in religion.

The unraveling of the One in religion began in the sixteenth century with the Reformation, and by the eighteenth century Western Christianity had become more divided than science could ever be. No one religious denomination gave people the basic values and beliefs with which most people thought about themselves and their relations to each other and to the world. The adherents of each denomination believed in the Parmenidean One, but they could not agree on who he was or, especially, how to worship him.

By bringing to the fore the possibility of choosing one denomination over another (or, eventually, one religion over another or no religion at all), the fracturing of religion fostered the development of things like the appeal to individual conscience in moral matters and the rise of democracy. Both of those are excellent things. Yet they result from the fact that human existence had become a patchwork of overlapping ways of understanding the world, a patchwork created by multiple sciences overlaid with multiple Christian denominations.

We rightfully laud many of the things that the modern period has given us. Those living in liberal democracies today are glad to be able to choose their religion rather than to have no choice or to not even know there is a choice. Most people in the world want the benefits that modern science offers, developments that make us and our families live longer and in more comfort than even the wealthiest royalty did two or three hundred years ago, or even a century ago. Many want to live in stable, participatory democracies with equal opportunities for all who live within them.

THE COLLAPSE OF THE ONE
AND THE DEATH OF "GOD"

All of those and many more good things are fruits of the modern period. But, at the same time, these divisions within science and its separation from religious thought meant that the One was fatally fractured. There was no longer a metaphysical unity holding Western European culture together.

The fracturing of the One began at least with the beginnings of modernism in the fifteenth century, but it was not noticed for a long time. It remained largely implicit until the late nineteenth or early twentieth century. Most people continued to act as if there were a One and to explain their lives and the world in terms of some One. Many still do.

Perhaps the first thinker to call our attention to its absence was Friedrich Nietzsche, born in 1844. Nietzsche is much maligned, often because of misinterpretations of his work. To be sure, he was not a Christian thinker. In fact, he explicitly thought of his work as anti-Christian. But if we think about the state of late nineteenth-century Western Christianity, to which he was responding, that may not be as awful a charge as it first seems. In any case, even if we decide that Nietzsche's thought is not only wrong, but dangerous, there is no better diagnostician of the ills of Western culture than he.

Nietzsche criticized Christendom—a term that means "the reign of Christian culture"—for having replaced genuine Christianity. Nietzsche did not distinguish between Christendom and Christianity, a mistake on his part, but his attack on Christendom nevertheless has a good deal to teach us. Nietzsche not only criticized Christendom for things like its hypocrisy, but he said that though it had once helped human beings to live full lives, it had outlived its usefulness. In fact, perhaps because he conflated Christendom and Christianity, Nietzsche couldn't see how Christianity was any longer possible. He believed that it had once given purpose to humanity, but as it had gained political and cultural power and become Christendom, Christianity had become something people professed, sometimes even passionately, but no longer took seriously:

Though the One had given Western culture its metaphysical unity from antiquity, that unity had been lost by the twentieth century.

Your faces have always been more damaging to your faith than our [the atheists'] reasons [for not believing] have! If the message of your Bible were written on your faces, you wouldn't need to insist in such a stubborn, demanding way on the authority of that book. A new Bible would constantly arise in you. But all your apologies for Christendom have their roots in your lack of Christianity; with your defense, you write your own indictment.[13]

Christians, he says, insist that they believe, but their lives don't show it. Christianity, he says, is merely our culture, no longer genuinely our faith, but it no longer works as a culture either: it is neither faith nor culture. Nietzsche's evaluation of the West and his criticism of it are damning.

Today most people know Nietzsche best, perhaps, for the claim "God is dead," made by a character he calls a madman in one of his parables. The claim is provocative, but the point of the parable in which we find it is twofold. First, it is to call our attention to the death of the One, to the fact that no meta-

---

13. Friedrich Nietzsche, *Human, All Too Human II* (1879), §405.

24

physical center holds European morality and culture together anymore. Second, and at least as important, the point of the parable is to get us to recognize the tragedy of that so-called death.

Speaking of God as he and those of his time understood him (that is, as the One), Nietzsche's madman says:

> Nietzsche makes the fracturing of the West's metaphysical unity clear: "God is dead"; we need a new principle for life.

> We are all his murderers. But how did we do this? How were we able to drink up the sea? Who gave us the sponge to wipe away the entire horizon? . . . Are we not continually falling? And backwards, sidewards, forwards, in all directions? Is there still an up and a down? Aren't we straying as though through an infinite nothing? Isn't empty space breathing at us? Hasn't it gotten colder? Isn't night and more night coming again and again?[14]

Many take this parable to tell us, as Clarence, a character in John Updike's *In the Beauty of the Lilies*, says, of an inexorable tidal wave of atheism and scientism cresting "in mad Nietzsche and sickly Darwin and boil-plagued Marx" that has wiped the shores clean of religion.[15] But I think that reading is a mistake—and even if it is right about how to understand Nietzsche, it is wrong about history: "today almost nobody speaks of an imminent 'extinction' of religions or of the religious any longer,"[16]

---

14. Friedrich Nietzsche, *The Gay Science* (1882), §125.
15. John Updike, *In the Beauty of the Lilies* (New York: Random House, 2003), 15–16.
16. Michael Reder and Josef Schmidt, "Habermas and Religion," in Jürgen Habermas et al., *An Awareness of What Is Missing: Faith and Reason in a Post-Secular Age*, trans. Ciaran Cronin (Cambridge: Polity, 2010), 2.

though for a while, especially in the first half of the twentieth century, many thinkers did. Today perhaps fewer people in North America and Europe attend church regularly,[17] but globally that doesn't seem to be true. If anything, academic interest in religion is also on the increase.[18] But as I said, I don't understand Nietzsche to be talking about the extinction of religion. Instead, his parable is a call to action: the One has fragmented and no longer works for us; it is dead, even though many of us pretend it is not (thus the many permutations of contemporary religion). Nietzsche's voice is that of someone who sees a tragedy but doesn't know how to respond. If we are not self-deceived, he says anxiously, we must *do* something because without the One we find ourselves disoriented and in the dark.

In spite of, and sometimes because of, our technological advancement, as the genocidal mass murders of the twentieth century show so starkly, Nietzsche's diagnosis is a good description of much of the last one-hundred-plus years: morally disoriented and in the existential dark.

Nietzsche's critique of the One was not just a criticism of the Christendom he saw around him. More directly, it was a criticism of the metaphysical foundation of Western thought, religious or otherwise, namely the One. As such, his work brought the entire philosophical project of modernism into question, the project of giving a rational, objective foundation to *all* belief and knowledge.

---

17. See C. Kirk Hadaway and Penny Long Marler, "How Many Americans Attend Worship Each Week? An Alternative Approach to Measurement," *Journal for the Scientific Study of Religion* 44, no. 3 (2005): 307–22.
18. See, for example, Jacques Derrida and Gianni Vattimo, ed., *Religion* (Stanford, CA: Stanford University Press, 1998). See also the 796-page volume *Political Theologies: Public Religions in a Post-Secular World*, ed. Hent de Vries and Lawrence E. Sullivan (New York: Fordham University Press, 2006), and the slim collection by Habermas et al., *An Awareness of What Is Missing* (see n. 16 above).

Nietzsche said, "There are no facts, only interpretations," a direct attack on the modern understanding of the world, including but not limited to religion. If detached, rationalist objectivity, the goal of modernism, is impossible, reduced to nothing more than one more interpretation of the world, what becomes of truth? If modernism is wrong about the objectivity of knowledge, is there any way to understand things like value except in relativistic terms, as the preferences of this or that community perhaps, or as merely the outcome of Darwinian forces that could have—and may have—taken another route? If there is no One grounding and giving unity to value as well as knowledge, what sense can a religious person make of her belief in God? Is it anything more than an irrational belief or perhaps an emotional coping mechanism? Rational objectivity was the goal of modernism. With Nietzsche, it becomes impossible for any of the highest human values. It's as if he turns Dostoevsky's question on its head: if there is no One, how can there be any values at all?

Not very many are Nietzscheans today, yet as Updike reminds us, Nietzsche managed to turn the world of ideas upside down a little

> We cannot escape dealing with Nietzsche's criticisms of the modern world as a whole.

more than one hundred years ago. Nowadays much thinking about religion is done in light of Nietzsche's critique of the One and its attendant morality and science. Almost every theologian is critical of modernism.[19]

---

19. Some of these are obvious, such as the liberation theologians (e.g., Gustavo Gutiérrez) and feminist theologians (e.g., Rosemary Radford Ruether and Elizabeth A. Johnson). European theologians influenced by the twentieth-century German thinker Martin Heidegger (e.g., Karl Rahner, Max Müller, and Jean-Luc Marion) are also obvious. But the dissatisfaction

Philosophers and theologians must worry not just about how to ground morality in the absence of the traditional God, but also about what the absence of a metaphysical foundation for our culture means in general. Whatever else those who follow intellectual pursuits today think, they cannot ignore Nietzsche's criticism; in some way or another, we have to take account of and respond to it.

As I said earlier, I think that Joseph Smith's teachings were a response to Nietzsche's criticism before Nietzsche made it; *avant la lettre* the latter-day restoration was ready to respond. But Latter-day Saints have yet to explore the possibilities that Joseph Smith's revelations offer to make sense of God, morality, and cultural values without relying on the metaphysics of the One. To the degree that we continue to implicitly and unconsciously rely on a theology founded on the metaphysics of the One, we too are subject to Nietzsche's criticisms.

> The teachings of Joseph Smith avoid Nietzsche's criticisms of Christianity, but Latter-day Saints have yet to explore that alternative.

with modernism is found also in less obvious thinkers, such as John Howard Yoder, Pope John Paul II, Stanley Hauerwas, and Catherine Pickstock.

CHAPTER TWO

Doing Theology before and after Nietzsche: We Have No Need to Fear Multiplicity

As I stated earlier, not everyone wants to do theology and almost no one needs to. But what does the lingering metaphysics of the One in Western thought and culture mean for Latter-day Saints who want to do theology or who find themselves in a situation where they need to? A great deal.

Much of the philosophical and sociological thinking and investigation of the last century was a response to the death of the One, to the fact that there was no longer a metaphysical unity holding together Western European culture and the spread of that culture across the globe through colonialization. Those responses resulted in attempts to understand that absence, attempts to describe it, and attempts to suggest alternatives, whether a revival of the old One, a new One, or a way forward without the One. Yet often these thinkers made those attempts by denying the One in one form only to bring it back in another.

TAKING JOSEPH SMITH'S REVELATIONS SERIOUSLY

In contrast to the Parmenidean aspects of Christianity, almost forty years before Nietzsche's madman announces the death of the One, Joseph Smith's revelations tell us that if we think of God in terms of the One—in other words, of God as an unembodied metaphysical being—then we do not understand who we are, much less who God is. Joseph does not preach a religion of the One.

Yet the truth is that Latter-day Saints seldom take seriously the opportunity that Joseph Smith's teachings present. For the most part, though we give lip service to what we learn from his revelations and insights, when we do theology, whether formally or, especially, informally, we continue to use the terms that are given to us by our broader culture. As a reflex rather than as the result of a thoughtful decision, we continue to think in terms of the One we have inherited from American religious culture (particularly Protestantism).

> A religion without a One is revealed to Joseph Smith; the God revealed by Joseph Smith is not a Parmenidean One.

For most of Latter-day Saint history, our thinking about religion has been dominated by the ways in which traditional theology and the philosophy of religion have thought about God, often even when we believe that we are explaining how we are different. The early Latter-day Saint converts brought the metaphysics of the One with them, particularly from Protestantism. The concepts of traditional, Protestant Christianity were the theological currency of their time, and Latter-day Saints used them even when they thought they were arguing for something different.

As a result, Latter-day Saints find themselves in a position somewhat like that of first-century Christian thinkers: though virtually invisible to us, the failed metaphysical One is so entwined in the way our culture thinks about everything, and especially in how it thinks about God, that we often invoke it or assume it without even knowing that we are doing so. Since those are the concepts the culture around us usually uses to think about God, we find it difficult not to use the same concepts.

Thus, when we try to reflect on our beliefs philosophically or theologically, we tend to understand the teachings of the Restoration from Joseph Smith to the present in terms of Western religious culture rather than understanding what the ongoing process of the Restoration has given Latter-day Saint culture. In spite of the intellectual and social upheaval resulting from the death of the One, its shadow continues to hover over us, perhaps as much as it hovers over the broader culture. For example, when we think about divine attributes, we often adopt the understanding of terms like *perfection* that we have inherited from that culture. We don't ask questions like, "Is perfection what those who think of God in Parmenidean terms think it is?" or "Does 'all power' mean for us what it means for God as the One?" or "What do the scriptures mean by 'eternal'? Do they mean what theologians mean when they talk in terms of the One?" Philosophers have long asked about "the problem of evil": How can an all-powerful, all-knowing, and all-loving God allow evil? Perhaps when we tackle that question, our difficulties may be the implicit result of thinking of God as a metaphysical One: as unembodied, outside time and space, et cetera; beyond being and nonbeing. Perhaps understanding the implications of worshipping an embodied relational divinity as revealed by Joseph Smith would untangle some of these theological problems. Or perhaps they would bring us up against new questions. Without exploring his revelations seriously, we cannot know.

That raises the question, How can we reflect on divine things without our thinking being implicitly structured by the One, which Joseph Smith's revelations reject—but without rejecting intellectual reflection on what we have been given or without refusing to offer explanations of our beliefs? How do we explain our religion without simply taking up fideism (a reliance on faith alone, without recourse to reason)? Is that possible? How can it be done? What is the best way to understand God intellectually in light of Joseph

> In spite of what Joseph Smith revealed, we continue to implicitly think in ways we receive from the tradition of the One, especially when we think about our Father in Heaven.

Smith's teachings? The answer isn't obvious, especially if we start with the dominant, Parmenidean assumptions our culture has about religion and divine things.

For twenty-five hundred years or so, the resource for those kinds of reflections has been philosophy, the use of reason to decide conceptual questions. There is a real question whether and how much we need to think about the Restoration with the tools of philosophy at all, a question about whether we need to do theology. There is nothing wrong with doing either of those, any more than there is with doing biology or history or business or theater. But no one needs to study any of those things to live a full life. Pursuits like philosophy and theology can be wonderfully enriching, to be sure, but they aren't essential to every person's life. Some people need to do them, but not everyone does. And no one needs them for exaltation. As the lives of very many good but nonphilosophical people across millennia prove, the scriptures, the prophets, and the practices of the Church of Jesus Christ are enough for both full life and exaltation.

Yet sometimes questions arise that niggle at our testimonies or challenge them head on, and sometimes, like early Christians, we need to explain ourselves not only to ourselves but also to others who sincerely desire to understand. We can rarely satisfy our critics. Occasionally we may need to defend ourselves against attacks on our beliefs, but our defenses are unlikely to change our critics' minds. In spite of that, often we need to be able to give explanations to those who are willing to listen and understand, whether inside the Church or out. At those times we cannot avoid doing philosophy and its twin, theology. We are unlikely to settle our friends' questions or our doctrinal differences with philosophical and theological tools alone. But, like early Christians, we can try to show that our beliefs make sense using the concepts at hand. The tools of reason may help us see for ourselves and show others the strength of the teachings of our tradition. The tools of reason can help us discover the truth.

> Obviously, neither philosophy nor theology is essential to religious life, but they can help us clarify our beliefs and find their strengths.

TRUTH

The word *truth* can mean a variety of things. We tend to think in terms of absolute statements, things one can say that remain the same regardless of time, circumstance, or person. Surely the truth that Jesus is the Christ, the Messiah anointed to bring salvation to all, is an absolute truth. It isn't true at one time and not true at another or true for one person but not another. Jesus himself says, "I am the way, the truth, and the life" (John 14:6). But notice that Jesus says *he*—the person, rather than what one can say about him—is the truth. That's hard to understand because we think of truth in terms of statements, and most commonly we understand true statements to be those that correspond to the way things in the world are: true propositions are those that represent the objective world accurately. Obviously that's a legitimate way of thinking about truth. I can say, "The Church of Jesus Christ of Latter-day Saints was founded in New York state in the United States in 1830," and that is true. It isn't going to change.

Nevertheless, that cannot be the way Jesus is thinking when he says he is the truth. What can he mean by that claim to *be* the truth? I think he is telling us that he shows us how we can go to the Father, that he is the manifestation of the Father, and that he reveals the life one must live in order to be with the Father. That's why he ends John 14:6 with "No man cometh unto the Father, but by me." Jesus describes himself in terms of how he is related to the Father and how he shows us our possible relationship; he shows how he stands as Revealer and Mediator between us and the Father. He is the truth because of the relationships he has to others, not because some statement corresponds to him. That is an old sense of *true*. A door can be true—or we can true it. When we say that, we are talking about the door's relationship to things around it. In relation to them, it is perpendicular and straight, or we can put it into that relationship.

There are still other meanings of the word *true*. A blacksmith might speak of true temper in the steel he has worked, meaning that the steel is unlikely to break. We also sometimes speak of true colors, meaning that they are not prone to fade. A person can be true by being faithful or loyal: "He was true to her while she was on her mission," "They were true patriots." In the nineteenth century and early twentieth century, the word was used to describe a virtuous person, as when someone said, "She was kinder and truer than anyone I knew." And we might describe a person as true and mean that the person speaks truly. The point is that if we talk about truth we should be clear what sense of truth we have in mind. Are we talking about the way statements correspond to states of affairs, about how something reveals something else, about what kind of relationship a person has with other persons, or about what a person reveals about what is most important? Of these, the first—how statements correspond to the world—is the least important (as important as it is and as often as it is ignored). The truth of relationship is even more important in the long run than the truth of statements. Yet it is the latter we most often concern ourselves with when we talk about truth.

And when we think of truth merely as the truth of statements—what we often refer to as "objective truth," or the truth having to do with objects rather than persons—we tend to think about truth in terms of progress. It's as if we learn certain true statements and then, over time, we refine those truths, improving them and replacing some, learning new truths as we go along. If that's the way things are, then the end goal is *the Truth*, the final truth, the final thing that can be said about something. At least in principle, the ultimate goal is a state of pure transparency, where we can see, in other words know, everything about everything. That's the dream of the Parmenidean One. Perhaps in the sciences such a goal makes sense as a working assumption, though even there I'm dubious. In any case, it doesn't make much sense in most other human endeavors, endeavors where rather than the One we find a multiplicity—an eternal multiplicity according to Joseph Smith's teachings. Consider the small world of marriage, constituted by two rather than only one. In that world that is necessarily multiple, there is no final thing to be said about my relationship to Janice, the woman to whom I am married.

Presumably we will continue to grow and change. If so, what we can say about each other will also grow and change, and there's no reason to assume that there will be an end to that change.

PROGRESS?

There's also no reason to assume that all change is either progress or regress. Presumably our relationship in the eternities will continue and as we have new experiences our relationship will change, though it won't necessarily be getting either better or worse. Our relationship could change over time, remain true, and yet not progress. Perhaps progress and regress are categories that don't make sense in some relationships. It seems to me that thinking that truth necessarily progresses confuses truth with technological development. It makes sense to say that there has been technological progress. Surely most people today are better off technologically than we were five hundred years ago. We have better ways to treat disease than we did then, though we have not yet been able to make those as widely available as we should. We can see into space much, much farther than we could anciently. We move about the planet and communicate with one another so much better than we did. It would be difficult to deny the truth that technology progresses.

It makes some sense to think that in spite of political difficulties in many places, many communities have made political progress, itself perhaps a kind of technological process, the technology of governing and being governed. Whatever the difficulties we now deal with, those living in representative democracies are better off than those who are not. We are absolutely better off with the abolition of slavery than we were when it was not only real (as it too often continues to be), but legal. Democracies are better off allowing not just those with property to vote, but all adults. And Westerners cannot deny that women's suffrage and the civil rights movement have been good things.

Many are free to choose their religion today, or to have none if they so feel. That is better than when states have attempted to decide the religion of all their inhabitants, or than when, in highly homogenous communities, only a relatively few people could imagine anything other than the religion in which they were raised and, so, were deprived of choice simply because no alternative existed for them.

But whether our political, social, and technological progress also mean that we have made moral progress remains a question. Matters of political and social change are inextricably entangled with morality, yet I don't believe that technological and political progress show that we are fundamentally better or morally different from those who lived a thousand years ago or more. Perhaps Europe has less war now than it did in the fourteenth century, for example. But that is complicated. It isn't obvious that there is less war globally, nor even how one would decide, and the wars of the twentieth century probably killed more people than many of the previous wars put together, perhaps even more than the conquest of the Americas. How do we decide which enormity is worse?

In general, do people show more respect for each other than they did several hundred years ago? That, too, is not clear. The answer partly depends on where you live. It may depend on what counts as respect in your culture. But the scandals in the United States surrounding the way politicians, artists, Hollywood moguls, and professors have exploited their workers, colleagues, and students for years and even generations make me think perhaps we have not.

At the individual level, worldwide we are beset by the same temptations and moral difficulties that have plagued human beings from the beginning. Technology has done nothing to reduce our lust, gluttony, avarice, sloth, anger, envy, or pride. In fact, those with access to technology have the new temptations that technological progress has brought, from a monstrous expansion of the pornographic exploitation of children and women to the isolation from others often created by our use of cell phones.

> Over the last five hundred years, humanity has made definite technological and some political progress, but not theological and perhaps not moral progress.

More to the point of this discussion, though, have religious thinkers made theological progress along with our technological progress? The idea of progress assumes that there is a final point toward which our ideas are tending, a conceptual or metaphysical Parmenidean One toward which we are progressing. Nineteenth-century Protestantism often thought in something like those terms, put very broadly as follows: early Catholic thinkers were improved on by later Catholic thinkers, whose theological imperfections were corrected by the Protestant Reformation. Sometimes Latter-day Saints have taken up the same view, seeing the restoration of The Church of Jesus Christ of Latter-day Saints as the culmination of that progress.

But suppose we understand the restoration of the Church in terms of dispensations—times when the gospel has been dispensed to those on the earth by an authorized servant with priesthood keys.[1] Though the final dispensation contains every-

---

1. See "Dispensation," https://www.churchofjesuschrist.org/study/scriptures/gs/dispensation.

thing given in any previous dispensation as well as new revelation, each of the previous dispensations—such as that of Adam, of Enoch, and of Jesus during his life on earth—had the full gospel even if in its own way. The people of the Book of Mormon had the fullness of the gospel even if, as appears to be the case, they didn't know about the three degrees of glory in the afterlife. That suggests to me that we ought not to understand the movement of the gospel from one dispensation to another in terms of progress.

THE FULLNESS OF TRUTH

If we think in the way I have described, having the fullness of truth doesn't mean knowing, finally, a One. It isn't finally knowing the last thing to be said about something—in this case, whatever it is that we presume (with Parmenides) makes each thing in the universe what it is and gives the universe its unity. The truth of which Jesus taught us is the truth that he reveals: how to get to the Father, that we can see the Father in him, and that he lives the life we will live if we love the Father. But *that* truth isn't reducible to one particular set of propositions, because it is a truth of relationship and life. It is a truth we live, whether we can put it into statements or not.

If Adam had the fullness of the gospel, and so did each subsequent dispensation, then presumably the reflections on the gospel of each of those dispensations were as adequate as our own. Yet the variety of ways we see prophets and others writing in the Hebrew Bible, the New Testament, the Book of

> The fullness of truth means an ongoing and full relationship with God that is expressed in different, ongoing ways.

Mormon, the Book of Abraham, the Book of Moses, the Doctrine and Covenants, and in Joseph Smith—History shows that their reflections on what they received by revelation were not the same as ours. Abraham, Moses, and Isaiah write very differently from one another, using different genres of writing, talking about and emphasizing different things. Each teaches the same good news (news about Jesus Christ rather than a metaphysical doctrine); each teaches that good news differently.

Few writers in the Book of Mormon write like those in either the Hebrew Bible or the New Testament. And Joseph Smith writes different things in different ways from any of the others. The same is true today: the living prophets and apostles preach differently than do those in scripture. They teach differently than did the prophets of the nineteenth and twentieth centuries. It's the same gospel, the same good news that salvation from death in all its forms is possible; the gospel isn't changing for the better over time even though it is understood and explained differently from one time to another. Part of the challenge of reading scripture is recognizing the differences between its ways of thinking and talking about things and ours, and then learning from that comparison. That should not be surprising, though.

To see why we ought to expect differences of many kinds between the various writings of scripture, think about our relationships with our loved ones in mortality. The question of how to write about what God has revealed is like the question of how I best express my love for my wife and children. The answer is this: by the ways in which I relate to them, by the things I *do* in those relationships more than by the things I say. That would be true even if I were someone very skilled in talking about families and family relationships, someone like a professor of family life.

It is sometimes reasonable or even necessary for every parent to step back mentally so as to think about those relationships, to give an account of them. I say to one of my children, "I love you because . . ." When I do that, though, I am not giving a final account. Instead, it's an account appropriate to the circumstances that gave rise to it. So I said different things to my children when they were toddlers than when they were teenagers, and I say yet different things to them now that they are adults. I also say different things to one child than I say to another, and different things to the same child in different circumstances. There is no one way of saying or explaining what our relationships mean. There is one love at work, one relationship, but no one way to speak it with finality. Love has to be said over and over again in a variety of ways and deeds, yet it is recognizable as love in every one of its expressions. In relationships truth is the truth of the relationship itself, of what happens in that relationship, not the truth of what we say about it. If we say true things about a relationship, we can do so because we live in it truly, and what we say truly at one time about it may be different from what we say at another even though we continue to live in the relationship truly. Scripture is like that. It is what a prophet, living truly in his relationship to the Father, can say about that true relationship as it pertains to us. What a particular prophet says to express his and our relationship may not always be the same. It may be different from what another one says. But it will be held together by the truth of the relationship, a unity of relationship that is anything but the unity of the metaphysical One.

The different ways the writers of scripture have for reflecting on, talking about, and explaining our relationship with God suggest that there is no one, final way of being in or reflecting on that relationship.

JESUS AS THE TRUTH

When Jesus says, "I am the way, the truth, and the life" (John 14:6), I think he implies that our ongoing relationship with him may or may not result in rational reflection. We may not do philosophy of religion or theology in response to our life with him. But our relationship is not meaningless if we do not. His way—the path he marks for us—and the truth are the same. His *life*, his way of being, is the truth to which we owe fealty, not the things we would say if we tried to describe his life or to think about it philosophically. That is the first point I think any Latter-day Saint theology must include.

That doesn't mean we ought not to think about our relationships either with others or with God propositionally. But it does mean that such thinking cannot be primary. Philosophical and theological reflection on Christianity depend on the truth of Jesus's life. That is the truth that theology should teach. But his life was not and is not a static thing.

> The truth of the gospel is the person Jesus the Messiah, not a set of propositions.

He lived; he continues to live. His life is ongoing and shows itself in a variety of ways through our lives. That means that if we think about Jesus's relationship with us reflectively, we are likely to find ourselves saying different things on different occasions and at different times as we try to express what that life means in those occasions and circumstances.

It doesn't follow that there is no truth. Anything but! There is truth, one truth, the truth circumscribed in the person Jesus Christ. *He* is the truth, but what we say about him is never more than a reflection of the particular circumstances in which we speak of him and the relationship that we have with him at that moment. What we say about our relationship to the members of the Godhead is like what we say about our relationships to our children. It is founded in our relationships, but never exhaustive of them. It requires that we speak differently at one time than we do at another. Sometimes silent companionship will be the best expression of that relationship, as it often is with a mortal loved one, as it often is in prayer.

Some might say that I'm arguing for mysticism, the idea that our relationship with God cannot be described. Perhaps I am. Whether I am depends greatly on what we mean by the word *mysticism*. But regardless, I'm not arguing that we cannot describe or express our relationship at all. I'm arguing two things:

Christ does not say, "Believe these things." He says, "Come unto me" (e.g., Matthew 11:28; John 7:37; 2 Nephi 26:25; 3 Nephi 9:14).

> First, I'm arguing that we express our relationship to God most fully in what we do rather than in what we say about that relationship.

We are told to believe *on him* (e.g., John 1:12; Acts 16:31; 2 Nephi 25:13; Alma 19:13; Doctrine and Covenants 35:2) rather than *in* a set of propositions.

Being a Christian is having a relationship to God and to others that results in seeing the world as a place that affords us opportunities to live in ways that we would not, could not, see otherwise. Seeing the world as God's creation and our stewardship means we live differently than if we don't see it that way. Seeing each person as a child of God and a potential god means that we treat people accordingly.

If our ways of living express the relationship we have with God, then we fully express what it means to be Christian, whether or not we can articulate our relationship and its meaning, whether or not our articulations of that relationship are up to the standards of this or that theology. When we understand the gospel of Jesus Christ by living its teachings, our Christianity is something that others can see and understand without need for further theological articulation. We say who we are and how we are related to the Father and the Son with our lives more than with our words.

That's what is behind my claim that there cannot be some final account or description of who God is or what he intends for us, though there are and must be accounts and descriptions adequate to the circumstances that call for them. Any reflection about our relationship with the Father can be understood only in the context of the circumstances in which it was uttered or written, in terms of the life it is revealing, whether the author is speaking authoritatively or is just someone talking about Latter-day Saint theology informally with a friend, and so on.

> As something we do rather than something we subscribe to, scripture study is one of the ways we discover and express our love for God. Scripture study is an act of worship and a form of theology.

SCRIPTURE STUDY AS THEOLOGY

The result of this understanding of how to talk about my relationship with God is that I see no better way to do theology than scripture study—the studying itself, not just the ideas, concepts, and principles that study finds in scripture.

But what about the particulars of my study? It isn't enough to say, "See, once again I have discovered that God loves me and that I must love others," even though, in fact, that is what I discover over and over again as I study scripture.

Joseph Smith is reported to have once said, "I have a key by which I understand the scriptures. I enquire what was the question which drew out the answer or caused Jesus to utter the parable."[2] I believe that is a general principle for interpretation: we understand a reflection on scripture or doctrine or practice only in relation to the question that brought about the thing we are interpreting. That may be a question in the text itself, or it may be a question that we have brought to scripture, or it may be a question that scriptures ask of those who read it. Our interpretations give voice to that question, but not always the same voice because we are not always the same. So: We can show what the scriptures perform, the invitation they make, by responding to the questions that arise when we study them carefully. With some of my colleagues, I call that "performative theology," a theology of what God does

Second, I'm also arguing that there is no final theology, because it is always done in response to a question, whether in the text, brought to the text, or generated by the text, and the questions change in changing circumstances.

---

2. Joseph Smith, *History*, 1838–1856, vol. D-1 [1 August 1842–1 July 1843], The Joseph Smith Papers, https://www.josephsmithpapers.org/paper -summary/history-1838-1856-volume-d-1-1-august-1842-1-july-1843 /102#source-note.

by speaking to us in scripture. I'll explain that term more fully later, but for now let's say that performative theology assumes that the scriptures enact something real—in particular Christ's loving invitation to come to him—and the job of theology is to help others hear the reality enacted by scripture.

CHAPTER THREE

A Few Doctrinal Claims: The Many without Anarchy

SOME THINGS WE BELIEVE

Even if you agree that scripture study is theology, there are times when a person must say something about Latter-day Saint belief and cannot just say, "Why don't we read Mosiah 4 together?" though he or she would like to. Sometimes Latter-day Saints have to give propositional descriptions of what they believe in spite of the fact that, ultimately, all theology is local, as I argued in the preface and in the last chapter. There are some general things one can say, things that differentiate the teachings of The Church of Jesus Christ of Latter-day Saints from those of other religions.

The things one could say don't sum up our beliefs as a church. There are sometimes surprising variations in what individual members or groups of members of the Church believe. (There's that local thing again.) Nevertheless, there are things that one can point to as common, though perhaps even then with variations. There might be variations in the specifics of how we make sense of them. Perhaps there are some that not everyone believes. But I think we can say there is a small set of beliefs that we expect those who are Latter-day Saints to share. So, before looking at one way of doing theology that takes account of its local and performative character, consider a few of those shared beliefs.

JESUS OF NAZARETH IS THE CHRIST

The first is something that all Christians accept:

> *Jesus Christ, the Son of God and divine himself, was born as a human being, lived a relatively short life during which he taught the good news of salvation, was executed on a cross by Roman authority, was buried in a tomb, and arose a resurrected being on the third day to sit at the right hand of God the Father in the full glory of his divinity.*

Without that belief, whatever someone makes of its particulars and however Christians might disagree about the meaning of some of those particulars, we cannot call ourselves Christian. That is crucial.

CONTINUING REVELATION

There are other beliefs, however, that make Latter-day Saints distinctive. One is a belief in prophetic continuing revelation:

> *God revealed himself to Joseph Smith, giving him revelations that initiated the Restoration. And he has continued to give revelation to subsequent prophets, as he did for ancient Israel.*

Theologically speaking, perhaps the most distinctive Latter-day Saint belief is found in Joseph Smith's revelation that there is a multiplicity of eternally existing beings. When we think about Latter-day Saint teachings, it is important to remember that most other Christian faiths, in fact almost all of them, teach that nothing exists besides God before his act of creation (not even time). Further, the world was not created from already-existing materials. It was created from nothing at all. It is not easy to understand what that means, perhaps no easier for our friends of other faiths than for us.

THERE IS NO PARMENIDEAN ONE

Our Christian friends can martial cogent arguments that explain what they believe; the belief in creation from nothing isn't simply irrational, as some Latter-day Saints are occasionally too quick to say. But no matter how rational traditional Christian belief might be and regardless of how much Latter-day Saints might learn from reading the work of traditional theologians, Joseph Smith teaches something else. In contrast with traditional belief, he teaches that matter is uncreated. In the King Follett sermon he teaches, "God had materials to organize from—chaos—chaotic matter—element had an existence from the time he had."[1] The stuff (a good word for primeval matter) from which the worlds were created is as eternal as God is; there is more than one eternally existing thing.

Joseph Smith says as well that the special kind of matter from which persons were created also existed from the beginning: "Man was also in the beginning with God" (Doctrine and Covenants 93:29), and "God never had power to create the spirit of man. . . . Intelligence is eternal and exists upon a self-existent principle."[2] As we see in the Pearl of Great Price (Moses 2:2; Abraham 4:1; compare Genesis 1:1), Creation was an organization of the preexisting chaotic stuff that was already at hand.

---

1. Stan Larson, "The King Follett Discourse: A Newly Amalgamated Text," *BYU Studies* 18, no. 2 (1978): 10–11.
2. Larson, "King Follett Discourse," 12.

Eternally, there are many; there never has been nor will be a Parmenidean One.

Within Judaism and Christianity, this is a radical claim, if not a unique one: that from which the cosmos was created, both personal and impersonal, existed prior to Creation, coeternal with God. Instead of a One that accounts for all that we experience (and is, at the same time, beyond experience), Latter-day Saints explicitly teach that there are multiple eternal entities interacting with one another.

This teaching, compared to the tradition that says God is the only uncreated being, ought to make a difference to the way Latter-day Saints see their world and their neighbors in it. It means that our Heavenly Father has never been alone:

> And the Lord said unto me: These two facts do exist, that there are two spirits, one being more intelligent than the other; there shall be another more intelligent than they; I am the Lord thy God, I am more intelligent than they all. . . . I dwell in the midst of them all; . . . I came down in the beginning in the midst of all the intelligences thou hast seen. (Abraham 3:19–21)

No intelligence is superior to God, but there were others besides him even in the beginning.

LOVE OVER WILL

Because God was not alone from the beginning, his relationship with us is not that of an absolute monarch bringing us into existence by fiat and then ruling by his arbitrary will, as some late medieval theologians seem to have believed. For most of the first thousand years or more of Christianity, God was not understood theologically as exercising arbitrary will. Instead, his person was understood as a complex balance of love and will. In the thirteenth century, however, a controversy arose over the relation of God to creation, and the outcome was William of Ockham's argument that God has absolute power, so much so that he can even contradict himself. His will is what makes him who he is.

> Whatever else we say about divine things, we can say that creation was not *ex nihilo* (from pure nonbeing); there has always been a multiplicity of eternally existing beings, as well as matter and intelligence.

For Ockham and many others subsequently, will took the place of love as the most obvious of God's attributes. In spite of Ockham's arguments, though, many such as the Franciscans continued to preach that our relationship to God is not determined by his will so much as by his love.[3] Latter-day teaching shares this early Christian and Franciscan view. The Father is absolute in several senses of that word, at least "supreme," "eternally self-sufficient," "complete or perfect," and "relevant to every situation." But he is not absolute in the sense that he depends on nothing else, can be affected by nothing else, and can will arbitrarily. Nothing is absolute in that sense.

Instead, God is unavoidably in relation with those with whom he is in covenant; he is affected by all of his children. He is a God of mercy, *ḥesed* in the Hebrew Bible, a word used for actions involving ongoing relations between persons,[4] as we see

---

3. For an excellent account of this shift, see Louis Dupré, "The New Meaning of Freedom," in *Passage to Modernity: An Essay in the Hermeneutics of Nature and Culture* (New Haven, CT: Yale University Press, 1993), 122–23.
4. Katharine Doob Sakenfeld, "Love: Old Testament," in David Noel Freedman,

God is not cut off from us metaphysically; he has been and will continue to be in active relationship with us, relationships that include emotion.

in such verses as Exodus 15:13: "Thou in thy mercy hast led forth the people which thou hast redeemed." He is a God of compassion: "Let thy tender mercies speedily prevent [meet] us: for we are brought very low" (Psalm 79:8). He mourns for our sins: "For the hurt of the daughter of my people am I hurt; I am black [I mourn in ashes]; astonishment [horror] hath taken hold on me" (Jeremiah 8:21).

Like his Father, Jesus Christ responds to us. He suffered for our sins in Gethsemane and on the cross (see Doctrine and Covenants 19:18). He weeps at our treatment of one another (see Moses 7:29, 37). He is easy to be entreated (see James 3:17; Luke 15:28). He loves us (see 1 John 4:8; Jude 1:21; Titus 3:4; Revelation 1:5).

AN EMBODIED GOD

Joseph Smith tells us, "If men do not understand the character of God, they do not comprehend their own character."[5] Hearing Joseph's teaching, someone might be tempted to think, "Surely when he says that he has in mind the moral character of God: if we do not understand his goodness, then we cannot understand what it means for a human being to be good." We can assume that is true. It is a feature of almost all Jewish and Christian belief about God: his goodness provides the measure for our own. That is the yardstick against which a Christian must measure any claim to human achievement.

ed., *The Anchor Yale Bible Dictionary* (New York: Doubleday, 1992), 4:377.

5.   Larson, "King Follett Discourse," 6.

But the surprise in the King Follett discourse, where Joseph Smith speaks those words about the need to know the divine character, is that he teaches less about God's goodness than he does about the kinds of things that set God apart from the Parmenidean One: in some important sense, God is the same kind of being we are. He says, "God Himself who sits enthroned in yonder heavens is a Man like unto one of yourselves. . . . [I]f you were to see Him today, you would see Him in all the person, image, fashion, and very form of a man, *like yourselves*."[6] Doctrine and Covenants 130:22 states, "The Father has a body of flesh and bones as tangible as man's; the Son also." That teaching is radically different from what we find in the Christian tradition. And that appears to be what the Prophet meant by *character* in the King Follett sermon, the thing we must understand if we are to understand ourselves.

At first glance it seems common sense for Joseph to say that the Father is a person like we are and that he has a tangible body. But it doesn't take much to start wondering what those claims mean, especially the second one, that the Father has a tangible body. After all, the bodies of the Father and Son can hover above us and are bright beyond description (see Joseph Smith History 1:17). Brigham Young and others taught that though their bodies are bodies of flesh and bone, the Father and the Son and beings like them do not have blood.[7] Luke 24:31 tells us that Christ can disappear from view immediately, and Luke 24:36 tells us that he can enter a room just as suddenly. Clearly, divine beings do not move through space as we do. Divine bodies are not like human bodies as we understand them. Nothing in our experience is embodied in that way. We must be careful when we assume that divine flesh is the same as human flesh.

---

6.   Larson, "King Follett Discourse," 7; emphasis in original.
7.   For example, Orson Pratt, "God Is Light, Etc," in *Journal of Discourses* (Liverpool: William Budge, 1878), 19:280–84.

Yet in spite of the difference between God's body and our own, there are things Latter-day Saints can say about divine bodies. At a minimum, they have a similar form or shape. Something with physical form has a physical boundary that differentiates it from another thing.

God has a physical body with a human form.

Most Christian theologies have been adamant that God is not a physical being. Christians and others often picture God as having a body—anthropomorphically, in human shape—but, most Christians say, that is only because a mental representation of God is impossible without giving him a shape like our own. It's the best we can do. To believe that God has a body is, according to the tradition, at best childish and at worst heretical. But Joseph Smith is emphatic about God's body. It has human form, and it is physical, "flesh and bones." It is "tangible": like our bodies, the body of the Father can be touched.

To say that a thing is tangible is to say that it is touch-*able*: it can be affected by the existence of some other physical thing. It can be acted on, be passive. Whatever else the body of the Father is like, it can be affected by other things, another radical departure from the tradition.

A TOUCHABLE GOD

By extension, having a material body, one that can be touched, suggests that God can also be touched in other ways. Embodied beings aren't affected by others merely mentally. The anguish I feel at a child's pain isn't merely mental. It is also physical. My body hurts in response to her pain, the same compassion the Hebrew Bible attributes to God. I am touched by the love of a friend not only mentally but physically. I feel good in his presence. Christ's vulnerability as a human being is a revelation of his divinity, of what it means to be God. That vulnerability is at the heart of what it means to imitate him. It is to be affected in body and soul.

In scripture we see the Father and the Son affected by others: caused to weep (see Moses 7:28, 37), caused to mourn (see Jeremiah 48:31), and caused to rejoice (see Zephaniah 3:17). Like us, the Father and the Son are emotionally touchable. In a movement that has grown since the end of the nineteenth century, today even many traditional Christians share that belief, though there has been some backlash.[8] To be embodied is to be affected. To be affected is to feel suffering, including the suffering of others.

If we think about the suffering in the world as a whole at any one time, the suffering of divine beings must be excruciating, though we can assume that it is ameliorated, perhaps even surpassed, by their relationships with those who love them. God's joy is eternally colored by his sorrow, as is our own, and I assume that his sorrow is eternally redeemed by his joy, as is ours—even if sorrow can never come to a complete end. For it to come to a complete end would require either that human beings no longer be agents or that God and those who become like him no longer be affected by other persons. Given Joseph Smith's other teachings, neither of those seems possible. As long as there is agency and as long as we can be affected by others, sorrow is possible—but so are joy and happiness (see 2 Nephi 2:11).

---

8. For Latter-day Saints, perhaps the best-known traditional Christian theologian arguing for God's embodiment is Stephen H. Webb. See his book *Jesus Christ, Eternal God: Heavenly Flesh and the Metaphysics of Matter* (Oxford: Oxford University Press, 2012). For an excellent essay setting forth the contemporary arguments for and against divine impassibility (by a proponent of passibility), see Charles Taliaferro, "The Passibility of God," *Religious Studies* 25, no. 2 (1989): 217–24.

A GOD OF POSSIBILITY

That both sorrow and joy are possible for divine beings reminds us of the wider point about divine materiality: God has possibility; things can be otherwise for him. That is another radical claim. Aristotle defined matter as such as possibility: to be material is to be able to change. But if so, then God can be otherwise—he can be here rather than there, for example. He has possibility if he is material. In scripture and revelation, God is a person for whom contingency—that things could be otherwise—is a positive rather than a negative way of being a person. Contingency is the essence of agency, whether divine or human.

In contrast, the God of the Christian tradition, understood as the Parmenidean One, has no possibility because he is not material. He cannot be otherwise than he is. Scripture portrays someone whose moral uprightness, his goodness, is constant and immoveable. He can be trusted absolutely because he will not be otherwise than upright and immoveable. But scripture also portrays someone who can be persuaded and change his mind (see, e.g., Genesis 18:20–33). In other words, the scriptures portray God as someone who has agency, whereas the Christian theological tradition says that agency pertains only to human beings. Supposedly, God is beyond agency because he is immaterial and, therefore, does not have possibility. Believing that he has a body changes that discussion considerably.

Of course, the view that God can be affected by others and be different in some respect at one time than he is at another is consonant with the way scripture portrays him. But to my knowledge no one outside The Church of Jesus Christ of Latter-day Saints has gone as far as did Joseph Smith in accepting the scriptural portrayal of God at face value and then following that portrayal to its conclusion.

MOTHER IN HEAVEN

Joseph Smith's willingness to accept the scriptural portrayal of God and follow its implications is especially obvious in the Prophet's affirmation that we have not only a Heavenly Father but also a Heavenly Mother. To speak of God as embodied is to speak of him, as the Prophet said, as "a Man like unto one of yourselves."[9] Embodiment means eternal multiplicity rather than the eternal unity of the One, and that multiplicity includes not only the multiplicity of individuals but presumably the kinds of differences that make us embodied beings, things such as perhaps skin color, height, and shape, as well as, and especially, defining characteristics like male/female multiplicity.

Our bodies are sexed bodies; the difference between the sexes is written in our eternal flesh. Part of the form shared by divine and mortal beings is sexual identity. So when the Prophet says that God is a Man like one of us, the word *man* is not merely a generic term for "person," though that usage was common in the nineteenth century. There is also a divine, eternal Woman. "Some early Latter-day Saint women recall that [Joseph Smith] taught them about a Mother in Heaven,"[10] and Latter-day Saints have recognized her existence from at least the middle of the nineteenth century.[11]

> We have not only a Heavenly Father but also a Heavenly Mother; we are sexed beings eternally.

9. Larson, "King Follett Discourse," 7.
10. The Church of Jesus Christ of Latter-day Saints, "Mother in Heaven," https://www.churchofjesuschrist.org/study/manual/gospel-topics-essays/mother-in-heaven.
11. See David L. Paulsen and Martin Pulido, "A Mother There: A Survey of

To talk about God in that way—as multiple, embodied, sexed—is to speak in a way that is radically different from what traditional Christianity teaches about divinity. In the tradition, the Father is usually portrayed not only as without body or parts but as also impassible, "pure spirit, invisible, without body, parts, or passions," to quote the seventeenth-century Westminster Confession, and "not passive in relation to other agents on the same level, not part of an *interactive* system,"[12] to quote the former Archbishop of Canterbury Rowan Williams. When the Christian tradition speaks of being without passions, it means "not capable of being passive, incapable of being affected by anything outside himself" (though, as mentioned earlier, there have been important arguments otherwise among traditional Christians).

> Central to a Latter-day Saint response to the death of the One and to our self-understanding is the truth that God is an embodied person with possibility, a sexed individual of flesh and bone, tangible both physically and emotionally.

Whatever else one can say about divine bodies, to say that God is embodied is to say that he (for Latter-day Saints, ultimately, they) is a person of real flesh and bone, even if that flesh and bone are quite different from our own: divine beings can move from one place to another (though they can do so in ways we don't understand), and they can be affected by others; divine beings have a

Historical Teachings about Mother in Heaven," *BYU Studies* 50, no. 1 (2011): 70–97.

12. Rowan Williams, *Christ the Heart of Creation* (London: Bloomsbury, 2018), 9.

form like ours, even in that they are sexual beings.[13] Though we don't understand the variations in human sexuality and that lack of understanding can be quite painful, eternal sexuality is at the heart of the Latter-day Saint understanding of families, divine and mortal.

THE UNITY OF THE GODHEAD

As I said in chapter 1, of course traditional Christians believe that Jesus was divine and that he was incarnated, a living human being. But they don't believe the Father is embodied and don't believe in Heavenly Mother at all. Latter-day Saints understand the unity of the Father and the Son, and presumably of all divine beings, as unity of purpose and understanding. But for those who believe in the traditional conception of the Trinity—most of Christianity—unity is more than that.

For them, the Incarnation is a complicated theological issue, a divine mystery. It is hubris for Latter-day Saints to dismiss their thinking about that issue as irrationality, as we sometimes do. One cannot read the writings of ancient and medieval thinkers like Augustine, Hildegard, and Aquinas or contemporary thinkers like Austin Farrer or his follower Rowan Williams without seeing the depth of their sincerity and their love for God. Nor can we merely dismiss their belief and thinking about that belief as mere superstition and self-contradiction. It is often surprising how much we can learn from them. But no matter how much respect we give the thinking of our brothers and sisters in

---

13. Since scripture as we have it today does not refer to Mother in Heaven, it consistently refers to God as "he," whether or not it is specifically referring to a particular member of the Godhead. For convenience's sake, I will do the same, though it runs the risk of undercutting Joseph Smith's prophetic understanding. Without contemporary prophetic guidance, Latter-day Saints do not yet have an easy way of talking about divinity that includes Joseph Smith's insight about Mother in Heaven.

the Christian tradition, it is clear that by comparison our claim about the embodiment of God is heretical—as is theirs from our point of view. They believe that the one being, God, ultimately is without body and, therefore, one in its very being. We believe that the several divine beings to whom the word *God* can refer are one in purpose, but not in being.

A GOD IN TIME?

Many Latter-day Saints have agreed with traditional Christians that God must be outside time. It is difficult to explain how he can have a "foreknowledge of all things" (Alma 13:7) if he is in time, so it is understandable that people would make that assumption. However, with few exceptions (such as Doctrine and Covenants 130:7) our scriptures consistently portray both the Father and the Son as beings existing not only in space as embodied beings but also in time. In Genesis 2 and 3, the Father walks and talks in the Garden of Eden with Adam and Eve, at a particular time in a particular place. Later Moses speaks with God at the burning bush and then face-to-face (see Exodus 3:2; 33:11), both events in time and space. The Father and the Son appear to Joseph Smith, above his head on a spring day (see Joseph Smith—History 1:17). Over and over scripture portrays God as part of temporal events.

Given how scripture portrays God, as well as Joseph Smith's revelations and what he teaches in the King Follett sermon about God's embodiment, we run a risk if we take the scriptural portrayal of him as inside time to be merely metaphorical. God's relationship to us is as an embodied being, and his embodiment is not just metaphorical; he exists in space. If his portrayal in scripture as an embodied being means that he has a real body, though not exactly the same as ours, I believe it is equally reasonable to believe that the scriptural portrayal of him in time suggests that he really is in time, though not necessarily in the same way we are.

In other words, if we accept that God is actually embodied rather than only metaphorically so, which I take to be doctrinal, we ought to be equally careful about assuming that his being in time is just a metaphor, that in spite of the scriptural portrayal of him in time, he is outside time. Just as his embodiment is different from our own, perhaps he has a different

> We do not know, but since the scriptures almost always portray God as existing in space and time and Joseph Smith talks of him in the same terms, it is reasonable to assume that, in some way or another, he is in time.

relationship to time than we do, but in scripture he is revealed as in time as well as space. Any arguments for God's having a body, in other words occupying space, are also arguments for his being in time. In fact, it is not clear what it means for an incarnate being to be outside time. How would he or she occupy space and yet also be outside time? A physical being in a timeless realm seems self-contradictory. The belief that there is some sense in which God is in time appears to be consonant with the other teachings of the Restoration.

WE CAN BECOME LIKE OUR HEAVENLY PARENTS

Perhaps even more important than understanding that God is embodied and has human form is the teaching that he is the kind of person we can become:

Some traditional theologies such as Eastern Orthodoxy share that belief (*theosis*). We see it even in Catholicism, for example in Thomas Aquinas.[14] And, there is the oft-quoted line from the Anglican C. S. Lewis: "It is a serious thing to live in a society of possible gods and goddesses, to remember that the dullest and most uninteresting person you talk to may one day be a creature which, if you saw it now, you would be strongly tempted to worship."[15] But what non-Latter-day Saint Christians mean by both parts of the claim, saying that we already have divine characteristics and that we can eventually become like God, is usually quite different from what Latter-day Saints believe.

We are already like and can become more like our Father and Mother in Heaven.

For other Christians, there is an important sense in which it is impossible to become like God. For them, the term *God* does not name a species of beings. It names the One who is perfection beyond being. So it makes sense for them to speak of becoming like God by being purified and perfected, but not by becoming a being in the same way that God is a being. Instead, they mean becoming, in some sense, perfected and *unified* with him.

For us perfection also means unification; in this we appear to agree with other Christians. Unity with the Father is what Jesus prayed for in John 17:20–23: "That they all may be one; as thou, Father, art in me, and I in thee, that they also may be one in us"

---

14. Thomas Aquinas, *Summa Theologiae*, III.1.2. For a good overview of the various ways of understanding theosis, see M. David Litwa, *Becoming Divine: An Introduction to Deification in Western Culture* (Eugene, OR: Cascade Books, 2013).

15. C. S. Lewis, *The Weight of Glory and Other Addresses*, rev. ed. (New York: Macmillan, Collier Books, 1980), 18.

(v. 21). We believe that our hearts and desires can be one with those of God. But our unity does not go beyond that: God is a being and each of us is a being, and that difference in our separate being will remain. For us being one also means becoming divine beings ourselves, though I think we must be honest about not really knowing what that means. Whatever it means, becoming a god oneself is unthinkable for traditional Christians.

In addition, for Latter-day Saints, unlike most traditional Christians (especially those after the Reformation), becoming like the Father is not an individual achievement. I cannot be saved alone. Through our conversion and our endowment, we are adopted by the Father into his family (see Romans 8:15–17). Through work on behalf of the dead in our temples, we make it possible for our ancestors also to be adopted into the same family. Only as members of God's family can we become like him.

SALVATION IS A FAMILY AFFAIR

Much of the import of the Prophet's teaching about divine embodiment is clear: Our life as embodied and sexed beings in families, beings for whom relationship and growth in relationships are central, is not just a feature of our earthly existence. It is not something that will disappear in the hereafter. Our life here is an imitation of the life of the divine Family; our familial relationship with God is not just a metaphor. Our families are not just signs of the kind of life we can live with God—they are the beginning of that life, the initiation here of what will continue there.

We are adopted as families into God's Family—and it is as part of that belief that our belief in Heavenly Mother is crucial. We imitate and initiate that Heavenly Family by being sealed to one another as husband and wife and children in a chain stretching backward to the beginning and forward to the Second Coming and, presumably, beyond. Our marriages can be eternal:

> If a man marry a wife by my word, which is my law, and by the new and everlasting covenant, . . . they shall pass by the angels, and the gods, which are set there, to their exaltation and glory in all things, as hath been sealed upon their heads, which glory shall be a fulness and a continuation of the seeds forever and ever. (Doctrine and Covenants 132:19)

Husbands and wives and their children can be sealed by priesthood authority in relationships that do not end with death. The same authority allows us to extend our family relationships beyond our immediate families to all of our ancestors. In God's temples we can do ordinance work that will allow them—if they wish it—to also be part of the great web of the Father's divine family: "neither can we without our dead be made perfect" (Doctrine and Covenants 128:15). Salvation in a vast web of familial relationships to each other and to our Heavenly Father and Heavenly Mother is available to any person who has ever lived.

> **Salvation is a familial rather than merely individual affair; ultimately it is an affair of the entire human family.**

By reminding us that marriage can be eternal, the 1995 Family Proclamation[16] reiterates Joseph Smith's teaching that our embodied individuality continues to exist in the hereafter and that our sexed bodies are

---

16. "The Family: A Proclamation to the World," https://www.churchofjesus christ.org/study/manual/the-family-a-proclamation-to-the-world/the -family-a-proclamation-to-the-world.

important to our individual and familial existence. Our relationships with our children can be eternal. Becoming like our Heavenly Parents involves being sealed to our spouses and children, and also being sealed to our ancestors.

FAITH, REPENTANCE, BAPTISM, AND THE GIFT OF THE HOLY GHOST

We believe that we must come to Christ (see, e.g., Matthew 11:28; John 7:37; 2 Nephi 26:25; 3 Nephi 9:14). And perhaps because we believe that we come to him as families more than as individuals, we also believe that coming to him requires more than a profession of faith in him. The resurrected Jesus says to the Nephites:

> And this is my doctrine, and it is the doctrine which the Father hath given unto me; . . . whoso believeth in me, and is baptized, the same shall be saved; and they are they who shall inherit the kingdom of God . . . ; and whoso believeth in me believeth in the Father also; and unto him will the Father bear record of me, for he will visit him with fire and with the Holy Ghost. . . . And again I say unto you, ye must repent, and become as a little child, and be baptized in my name, or ye can in nowise receive these things. . . .
>
> Verily, verily, I say unto you, that this is my doctrine, and whoso buildeth upon this buildeth upon my rock, and the gates of hell shall not prevail against them. And whoso shall declare more or less than this, and establish it for my doctrine, the same cometh of evil, and is not built upon my rock. (3 Nephi 11:32–40)

The usual way we précis this is: "faith, repentance, baptism, the gift of the Holy Ghost, and endurance to the end qualify us for the celestial kingdom."

Though most of the older Christian churches, such as Orthodox Christianity and Catholicism, teach the necessity and salvific power of ordinances (also called "rites" or "sacraments") like baptism, many Protestants today deny that necessity. Like those older churches, Latter-day Saints teach that certain ordinances are essential, and we practice baptism for the dead (conceptually not that different from the prayers for the dead that some Christians practice) to resolve the difficulties that the need for ordinances creates for those who die without the opportunity for authorized baptism.

> We come to Christ by faith and repentance, as well as by the ordinances of baptism and receiving the Holy Ghost; then we must endure to the end.

CHARITY

Finally, at least for this partial list of teachings, essential to our belief is this:

> *At the heart of the Christian story is the love that the Father and the Son have for us and that we should return to them and our fellows. Without that love we will, at best, gain the world and lose our soul—and the actual world.*

Jesus asks, "For what is a man profited, if he shall gain the whole world, and lose his own soul?" (Matthew 16:26). But he also tells us how to avoid that tragedy: "As the Father hath loved me, so have I loved you: continue ye in my love" (John 15:9). He continues, "This is my commandment, that ye love one another, as I have loved you" (John 15:12). That is the entire point of our existence, learning to love one another as God loves us, which means also loving God.

CONCLUSION

A few of the things that I've enumerated as taught by Latter-day Saints overlap with things believed in traditional Christianity. In particular, we share the belief that salvation comes only through Jesus Christ and that his love for us means that those who accept him must love as he did. In spite of that very important overlap, for the most part other Christians will find our beliefs shocking. However, with the possible exception of my claim about divine temporality, I think that any Latter-day Saint doctrinal theology (technically referred to as "dogmatic theology") would include at least the claims I have suggested.

Some doing theology may understand the claims differently than I do. Some may think that additional points must also be included. I might be persuaded. Perhaps easily. But even if I have overlooked something essential or important, my point is that only a few beliefs are fundamental to being a Latter-day Saint. Further, whatever one thinks is missing or insufficient about the things I've attributed to Latter-day Saint belief, most of the things I've listed are unquestionably things we could not say of the Parmenidean Eternal One. The basics of Latter-day Saint belief show that it is a religion of the Eternal Many.

However, this book is predicated on the belief that there is a better way for us to think about God and ourselves and our relation to God than by making lists of propositional statements of belief and then giving rational justifications for them. The-ology—full-throated God-talk—ought to be spiritual discipline more than mental exercise. And I take the word *discipline* in its root sense, "that which teaches us, making us disciples." Our daily practices, the love and service that make up pure religion (see James 1:27), will be different in quality if they are informed by spiritual discipline.

Where is that spiritual and mental discipline to be found? One place, though not the only place, is what I suggested in the previous chapter, in our relationship with scripture. (Other places are, for example, personal prayer, the sacrament, and temple worship. All these school our spirits and prepare us to work in God's kingdom as he calls us to serve. In that sense they are all theo-logy, talk with and by God.) The discipline of serious scripture *study* can open our hearts and minds so that we hear God's invitation to his love, and if we have heard and understood that invitation, our relationships with others will be informed by what we have learned.

> Potentially, careful scripture study is better theology than the logical explanation and analysis of doctrines (dogmatic theology) because the former is more likely than the latter to help us hear God's call to us.

The first advantage of scripture as a way of thinking and reflecting is that believers have had scripture and thought about it for longer than we have had philosophy and theology, much longer. When Hebrew and Christian religion encountered Greek thought and took up philosophy as a way of explaining itself, scripture had been being written and thought about for a thousand years or more. And that thinking did not stop with philosophy's entry on the scene. Scripture reading and response continued to run alongside dogmatic theological thought (in other words, philosophical thought within religion) long after the initial encounter, as we see in writers like Bede, Alcuin, and Bernard of Clairvaux, who wrote thoughtful commentary on scripture.

Scripture itself has been an alternative way of thinking for longer than we have had theology, though it has seldom been recognized as what it is, a genuine way of thinking about God and the world that is different from the way of dogmatic theology. Thinking that reveals itself through scripture can provide us with a different way of understanding the world and our place in it.

Rowan Williams says that the doctrines of Christianity "make sense, not first as an explanation of things but as a credible environment for action and imagination, a credible means of *connecting* narratives, practices, codes of behavior; they offer a world to live in."[17] I couldn't agree more, but what he says is twice true for scripture, which offers us a way of credibly connecting the variety of ways we inhabit the world so that our lives are whole and holy rather than fragmented and debased.

Our next chapter will take up one way of understanding theology as an enterprise of reading scripture closely.

---

17. Williams, *Christ the Heart of Creation*, xi.

CHAPTER FOUR

An Alternative (to) Theology: The Privilege of Scripture Study

NONDOGMATIC THEOLOGY?

As a brief look at the teachings of Joseph Smith showed us in chapter 3, he teaches a religion that is radically non-Parmenidean, opening a way for Latter-day Saints to respond to Nietzsche's criticism of the One and the crises of religion that have followed since.

Various Latter-day Saint theologies are possible, but however one goes about creating one, it cannot assume the Parmenidean One. It has to understand reality as eternally multiple from the ground up.

Given the history of theology, it is difficult to do theology without implicitly invoking the One. But *difficult* does not mean "impossible." So to those who wish to take up the work of creating dogmatic theologies of Latter-day Saint belief, I say, "Go ahead." If done by the Spirit and designed to promote love for others and for God, that work cannot be objectionable. But I have already suggested that there is a better way of doing theology than beginning with the list I've created here, or some other,

Latter-day Saint teaching offers a radical solution to the problem of the One by showing that its fragmentation is a blessing rather than a problem. That fragmentation opens up a space for a different way of thinking about God, the world, others, and ourselves—namely, a way in which the Many is fundamental, brought together in covenant.

and spinning and weaving from it a larger list of propositions that we ought to believe, making connections between them as we go, and demonstrating their plausibility.

I am hardly the first to be skeptical about dogmatic theology. Thinking about it in *Concluding Unscientific Postscript*, the great nineteenth-century Danish thinker Søren Kierkegaard offers a parable—in his usual acerbic way.[1] Paraphrased, it goes like this: Suppose someone said, "I haven't been a believer, but I did spend every hour of my life thinking about Christianity." Or suppose a person was accused of persecuting Christians, and the accused person responded, "I admit it. I have wanted nothing more than to root Christianity from the earth because I can see how powerful it is. It must be destroyed." Or suppose that another accuser said of someone else, "This person has renounced Christianity," and the accused person agreed: "It's true. I could see that it was all-or-nothing with Christianity, and I could not give it every part of me." And, finally, suppose a professor at the university came forward and said, "I am not like

1. Søren Kierkegaard, *Concluding Unscientific Postscript to the Philosophical Crumbs*, trans. Alastair Hannay (Cambridge: Cambridge University Press, 2009), 194–95.

those other three. I not only believed in Christianity, I reached the point where I could explain it. I have shown that what the apostles taught in the first century of the Christian church is only partly true, but I have also shown how there is a theological point of view from which it all makes sense and is the true truth."

Which of these four positions would be the most terrible? Kierkegaard asks. His answer is that no one's position would be as embarrassing as that of the professor in the parable, for whom Christianity is something objective, a topic to be analyzed and taught, rather than something that requires faith and risk.

In the twentieth century, the German theologian Rudolf Bultmann also worried about what happens when we try to think about or talk about God in the same ways we talk about ordinary objects.[2] It seems to be impossible to avoid doing that if we do theology dogmatically. As the contemporary philosopher of religion Jean-Yves Lacoste says, "We may be content with theoretical knowledge of such things as subatomic particles, but we could hardly be content to know that the proposition 'Jesus is Lord' is theoretically sound. But that is the most that theology can offer us."[3] Even if theology could give us proof that the claim "Jesus is Lord" is a theoretically sound claim—in other words, that it is consistent with the relevant evidence and logically productive of further generalizations—that is the most that theology could possibly do (and it probably cannot do that). But even if it could do that, it would hardly be enough to tell us what effect that claim should make on us, how we should respond to it, or what kind of praise the claim entails, the questions that are at the heart of religious conviction and experience.

---

2. Rudolf Bultmann, "Das Problem einer theologisches Exegese des Neuen Testaments," *Zwischen des Zeitens* 3 (1925): 334–57.

3. Jean-Yves Lacoste, *The Appearing of God*, trans. Oliver O'Donovan (Oxford: Oxford University Press, 2018), 179.

Does that mean that dogmatic theology, perhaps the dominant kind of theology since the age of Scholasticism (from approximately the twelfth century through about the seventeenth), is always guilty of something like idolatry, focusing its attention on a being made by human minds rather than on God himself? We have seen Kierkegaard implicitly argue something like that, and others have too, including me.[4] But I recanted shortly afterward, though the danger of idolatry in theology is a real danger.[5]

As much as I enjoy Kierkegaard's parable and as much as I am convinced he makes an important point with it, as irony often does, it goes too far. People like the professor—or Bultmann or other contemporary theologians—could not only offer their explanations of Christianity but also genuinely live the life of a Christian at the same time, and their explanations could accord with their lives. Rational explanation and real Christian life are not incompatible. Famously, Augustine and Anselm wrote theologies that were, for them and their students, not merely theoretical, though they are often studied as if they are. But even scholastic, dogmatic theologies, like those of Thomas Aquinas, are not necessarily incompatible with Christian life.

Nevertheless, dogmatic theology runs the danger of turning us into Kierkegaard's professor, of making us lukewarm rather than hot or cold (see Revelation 3:16). In principle, there's nothing wrong with doing dogmatic theology. In the end, though, in itself it is more an exercise of the imagination and intellect than

---

4. E.g., James E. Faulconer, "Why a Mormon Won't Drink Coffee but Might Have a Coke: The Atheological Character of The Church of Jesus Christ of Latter-day Saints," *Element* 2, no. 2 (2006): 21–37.

5. James E. Faulconer, "Rethinking Theology: The Shadow of the Apocalypse," in *Faith, Philosophy, Scripture* (Provo, UT: Neal A. Maxwell Institute for Religious Scholarship, 2010), 109–36.

a *spiritual* exercise and discipline when we most often need spiritual discipline.

PRACTICE OVER BELIEF

Of course, as I said earlier, no one needs to do theology; salvation is available without it, perhaps for some even more readily available without it. Unlike serving and comforting, loving and healing, theology will never count as one of the things one must do to be a follower of Jesus Christ. Yet there are times and occasions when we do theology, sometimes out of practical necessity, sometimes merely as part of the human desire to understand, which may be its own necessity.

In chapter 3 I made some suggestions about theology. The most important of them is that the truth of Christianity is the truth of the person Jesus Christ, rather than the truth of any set of propositions. From that personal truth flows the truth that our practices are more important than our beliefs. To the extent that our beliefs are important—and they often are—they are important because they form part of our meaning-ful practices. At the judgment bar, God is not going to tick off a series of questions about the orthodoxy of the beliefs we held, but he is going to be interested in the lives we led: the widow and orphan we comforted, the hungry we fed, the prisoners we visited, the ill we nursed. He is going to want to know how we have lived with his beloved brothers and sisters, his "little ones" (Matthew 10:42). The gospel truth is the truth of a *living* being. Because of that, theology will always have a

> Theology of whatever kind will always be secondary to a life of Christian charity. (I doubt that many will disagree.)

secondary place to acts and deeds, though it will not be irrelevant to those words and deeds.

But also, because Christ is living, continuing to work and to speak (see Moses 1:4), and because he is not an Eternal One and we neither are nor will be, when it comes to theology, at least in mortality, there is no one, final, all-encompassing explanation of divine things and our place in relationship to them. The many entities that there are continue to grow and change in their relationships, requiring ongoing, growing explanations. Another suggestion I made was that all theology is local. It happens in response to a particular question that arises in particular circumstances at a particular time for certain people rather than others.

SCRIPTURAL LANGUAGE AND REASON

In chapter 4, without much explanation, I proposed that if we are going to create theologies, the best ones happen when a person studies the scriptures—in other words, reflects on ancient and modern revelation—without assuming the Parmenidean One and the baggage that accompanies it. That is easy to say but harder to do than we often assume. We often associate scripture study with routine reading of scripture for a few minutes a day. That can be an important part of our daily worship, but it is not what I have in mind. Instead, I'm talking about a slow, careful, prayerful practice that is sometimes called "close reading."

When we think about theology, the temptation is to think that only the explicitly and formally rational thought of philosophy and theology can give us the tools for our reflection. That is a background assumption shared by almost anyone doing theology, whether a religious conservative or liberal, and someone accepting that assumption will think that my proposal about combining theology with scripture study sounds, perhaps, slightly nutty or at least implausible. The problem with my proposal is compounded by the fact that the leap from the criticisms I've made of the Christian theological tradition to scripture study as an answer to those problems for theology is not obvious. So before doing theology by close reading, step back a bit to see why I think scripture study is a legitimate way of doing theology.

The key is an insight that a number of twentieth- and twenty-first-century thinkers with names like Martin Buber, Hans Boersma, Jean Wahl, Jean-Yves Lacoste, Paul Ricoeur, Stephen Mulhall, Mark Wrathall, and Yoram Hazony have had: well-founded thinking and understanding don't occur only in the ways of formal logic and physical science. We can think in other ways, as presumably happens in scripture, and that thinking is not ungrounded or undisciplined simply because it isn't philosophy or dogmatic theology. There are multiple languages for talking and thinking about the world, and no one of them, such as physics or mathematics, is a master discourse into which all of the others can ultimately be translated.

A syllogism arguing for the autonomy of both religious and science discourses is simple:

> A good translation from one kind of discourse to another
> is possible only if they are about the same thing or things.
> Religion and science are not talking about the same things.
> So it is not possible to translate the insights of one into the
> other well.

As we will see, a syllogism of the same form could be constructed for other ways of talking about the world and our experience, for poetry and science, for example. Translations can be made from any language to another, but it doesn't follow that nothing important is lost in doing so. No one language can serve as the language into which any other can be translated without loss.

Because of the lack of fit between the language of science and logic, on the one hand, and the things of religion, on the other,

No one language is the "master language" for interpreting the world.

ultimately, insisting that in order to explain religion we must be able to give a formally rational account of it is like trying to pack a too-small suitcase: supposedly solve one conceptual problem here and another pokes out over there. Like our suitcase, reason—understood in the constricted, formal sense we usually give to it—cannot contain what we are trying to put into it. But that hardly means that there is nothing to that which we are trying to put in, nothing to our religious experience, practice, and knowledge. Believers shouldn't think that they can supposedly solve the problems between our faith and our intellect by throwing the latter out and concluding that religion is irrational and, then, further concluding that its irrationality is acceptable. Those who come to that conclusion are called fideists, and fideism is dangerous, especially to the young who may be unable to throw out their intellect in order merely to believe.

THE RICHNESS OF CREATION

Medieval Christian thinkers like Augustine understood this problem of needing to explain belief without being able to give the kind of account one finds in other areas of human thought. They saw it as a problem of language: Creation is thicker, richer, than any one expression of it can capture. The result of that richness, which they called "the superabundance of grace,"[6] in other

---

6. The phrase is a paraphrase of the topic of Romans 5:15–17. The notion of superabundance has been philosophically and theologically influential for more than a thousand years. The early Christian thinker Ambrose (fourth-century bishop of Milan) wrote a commentary on the superabundance of Creation, *Hexameron*. The sixth-century Roman Christian senator Boethius deduces from that superabundance that it is impossible for some-

words the overflowing of God's gift to us, is that at some point our language will fail to do justice to Creation. Sometimes that failure may even be manifest as contradiction. To recognize that isn't to resort to irrationality. It is to recognize that things are more interesting and complicated than any one language can, by itself, describe. The world isn't irrational, nor is religious belief; but when thinking about either, at some point we will be unable to do justice to what we see and know.

> The richness of the manifold world ensures that no single language will ever fully capture what we know by acquaintance and experience, though several can gesture toward it in various ways.

Early and medieval Christian thinkers believed that we must trust in—have faith in—our experience, including our experience with God, if we are to have knowledge. We must be willing to have faith in and rely on what we love. And we must be willing to put our love to the test; our faith must be tried if it is to be true faith. Thinking about our beliefs and practices is one way of putting our faith to the test, but our thinking about religion always begins in faith, is always founded in trust.

---

thing to have a nature that is equal to or better than its origin (Boethius, *Consolation of Philosophy* 3.10). Nietzsche later used the medieval idea as an analogy: music and myth have their origin in the superabundance of joy informed by pleasure and pain (Nietzsche, *Birth of Tragedy*, 24).

THE ANEMIA OF MODERNISM'S FAITH AND KNOWLEDGE

In contrast with older views of the relationship of faith and reason, modernism (especially beginning in the eighteenth century) has assumed that faith is an immature, uneducated way of understanding things. For moderns, faith isn't trust. It is weak belief, and this difference in how each understands faith always puts religion at a disadvantage in modern thinking. For moderns, the highest form of understanding is conceptual, and those who don't have conceptual understanding are immature, uneducated, unserious, or some combination of the three. So, when religious people say that their understanding is ultimately a matter of faith, they appear to many to be saying that it is a matter of ignorance, naiveté, or superstition.

> The modern view is that there is really only one language for talking about the world, that of objectivity, making faith into weak belief rather than trust, something for the immature and uneducated.

In place of the view that knowledge begins in loving trust, modernism insists that knowledge requires the rational construction of some aspect of an objective world. That shift in understanding moves us from the medieval understanding that faith is what makes knowledge possible to the modern understanding that faith is unfounded belief.

NONCONCEPTUAL UNDERSTANDING

Making a case for faith, then, means making a case against the modernist assumption about knowledge, that real knowledge is acquired by objectively deducing clear concepts. The case I propose will require us to ask about the nature of thought and expression:

1. Is there nonconceptual understanding?
2. How do we express something if it is nonconceptual?

My answers to those questions will be "yes" and "in many ways."

POETIC THOUGHT

First, is there nonconceptual understanding? Before we think about religious faith, let's think about another realm of human thought, poetry. Doing that will help us think about faith by helping us see another place that, analogously, is a matter of genuine knowledge but does not give us an objective description of the world.

We could say that poets think in poetry.[7] They don't first think in conceptual ways and then add meter and rhyme to those concepts, clothing their concepts in metaphor as they go.

> Poetry lets things appear to us that we might not otherwise see.

That's what mediocre poets do (*poetasters*, my English professor called them). It seems that poets understand things in language, but without having to begin conceptually.

---

7. My argument is related to the arguments I mentioned earlier, those of Buber, Boersma, Wahl, Lacoste, Ricoeur, Mulhall, Wrathall, and Hazony. In particular, I recommend Paul Ricoeur, *The Rule of Metaphor: Multidisciplinary Studies of the Creation of Meaning in Language*, trans. Robert Czerny (Toronto: University of Toronto Press, 1977). See especially Ricoeur's discussion of I. A. Richards's rhetoric: "Semantics and Rhetoric of Metaphor," 76–83.

There is a more careful way to put the point: like painters, poets use language to allow things in the world to show themselves to us. If I point to something I want another person to see, I allow it to appear to her by doing so. It shows itself to her by means of my pointing. The language of poets is similar, but it not only points to particular things in the world, it brings them to our experience. Poets don't just show us what they see.

Poetry makes a new experience of things and the world possible.

We aren't just looking at the world through their eyes, though that is part of what happens in the poem. Poets let the things they see show themselves to us through what they write, things and the relations of things to each other and to us. The poem gives us an experience of the world that we share with the poet rather than a vision of what the poet saw.

If that's what a poem does, then there is no reason to assume that a philosophical restatement of the poem would tell us what the poet really thought. And even if it did tell us that, the poem is about the things the poet experienced, not what she thought. So we cannot assume that an accurate philosophical restatement of the concepts we find in the poem reveals the same world in the same way that the poem does. When we understand the poem, our first level of understanding it is of the things and the relationships it reveals rather than the concepts it employs.

As an example, consider a fragment of a poem from the German romantic poet Friedrich Hölderlin. Two famous lines read, "In lovely blueness blooms / the steeple with its metal roof."[8] I recall vividly the first time I read those lines. I could never again

---

8. Friedrich Hölderlin, *Hymns and Fragments*, trans. Richard Sieburth (Princeton, NJ: Princeton University Press, 1984), 248–49. My translation.

see a Black Forest church in the mist of morning the same way. I had never seen the churches' blueness—particularly in the metal roofs, but also in the windows, even in the brick and mortar and plaster, regardless of their objective color. Perhaps painters see that blue, but I had not. Nor had I ever experienced a church steeple as blooming from the building rather than towering over everything around it. But in Hölderlin's lines, I did.

Used by Hölderlin, the word *blooms* brought the tower and its blue to me in a new way, for I had never before experienced the blue of the steeple and the steeple itself as something that happens, as an event in which I participate rather than only as the properties of an object that I observe. Reading the poem, I cease to be the center of things because the meaning of the poem is not what I find in it, but what it allows me to see in the world—the new world it allows me to be in.

Reading the lines from a fragment of a poem changed, if only in a small though moving way, how I experience the world. I use concepts to talk about having read the poem, what I understood. But the meaning of the poem is the possible experience and ways of relating to the world that it opens up more than the concepts it employs.

PROPHETIC THOUGHT

I would make a similar case for prophetic thinking, that it is often expressed in a peculiarly prophetic way, especially in those writings that are preserved for generations because they continue to be valuable to believers who read them. What is revealed through the writings of prophets is often not understood better by reducing it to philosophy or philosophically informed theology, as if the prophets were doing theology, but naively.

If poets think poetically in their poetry, we can also suggest that prophets think prophetically in their prophecy: they make it

> **Prophets make a new experience of things and the world possible, the experience and the world in which God reveals himself and into which he invites us.**

possible for the things they have received to show themselves—to be revealed—to us.

Prophecy opens a way of being related to God, other people, and the world by letting those things appear in the world differently than they did before. What we should see in the prophet's words is the world he reveals, not only what he thinks about that world. (We may never be able to know what an ancient prophet was thinking.) The prophet reveals the word and world of God, not simply things having to do with his own time and place—though he does the former only through the latter. The prophet can speak only in history, but prophecy always exceeds its history, and our primary interest as believers is in that excess.

There are sometimes good reasons for paraphrasing the words of the prophets, for explaining what they say in ordinary language, or for doing dogmatic theology using what they say. But when we do that, we are talking about concepts rather than about religious life, thinking about religion rather than living it; sometimes we may be confusing the conceptual content of what the prophets say with what they reveal through what they say.

The scriptures don't show us the one and only one way to understand that which they talk about. They show us one of the many ways it can be understood (but, of course, that there are many ways does not imply that every way is the truth). They help us see the richness and multiplicity of the world we live in and to see that multiplicity as God reveals it and as it reveals God.

The scriptures address me in my religious life, a life founded on trust; they are to help me remember things I may have forgotten and see things I've not yet seen. We should read them as texts that have something to reveal to us. That means preparing ourselves to receive what they offer.

> What shows itself through scripture is not a metaphysical One beyond human experience, but a many. It is many in that it reveals more than one thing in more than one way.

How do we do that? What does it take to give prophetic thought its due, to recognize it as a legitimate form of thought that doesn't have to be translated or reduced to some other kind of thought for us to understand it?

GIVING PROPHETIC THOUGHT ITS DUE: PERFORMATIVE THEOLOGY

We have known for a long time how to treat prophetic thought as a legitimate mode of thought in itself. Doing so has been part of the religious tradition, coming before and then running alongside the rational tradition, as long as we have had scripture. This is thinking that occurs by careful, slow reading that allows what we are reading to question us: close and reflective reading of prophetic thinking, usually of canonized scripture, with the assumption that it has something to reveal.[9]

---

9. My colleagues and I are hardly the first ones in the Church to advocate close reading of scripture. In the 70s through the 90s, Arthur Henry King, of BYU's English Department, taught close reading to many students, and we see instances of it in the work of people like John W. Welch and other pioneers of Book of Mormon study in the twentieth century. In particular, King and Welch showed us how to look closely at detailed rhetorical

> Scripture addresses me as someone living a religious life rather than as someone answering an intellectual question; prayerful close reading prepares me to hear it that way.

Close reading is a way of being taught. We cannot read without presuppositions, but we can do so with an attitude that allows our presuppositions to be put into question by what we read. That's the attitude of close reading. It is a way of listening to the Word in the word. The point is to discover how the theologian and her audience are invited to Christ when they don't just read but hear what the prophetic voice of scripture reveals about how to be oriented toward the world and God.

This makes for a different kind of theology, something that some friends and I call "performative theology." *Performative* is a term of art for philosophers who have noted that there is a kind of language they call "performative," language that performs or accomplishes something. For example, if a person with the right authority in the right circumstances says to a couple, "I now pronounce you husband and wife," those whom the authority addresses are, in virtue of those words and their effect, husband and wife. Those words have the power to make the couple what the words say they are.

As the name suggests, performative theology shows us that scripture brings about something.

---

features of scriptural texts. Welch is especially known for his work on chiasmus. We hope to add to the tradition coming from people like King and Welch rather than take away from it.

Commands and promises are also examples. A parent who says to a child, "Do the dishes," is not just making a statement; she is performing an act, the act of commanding. "Do the dishes" is different from merely saying "Someone should do the dishes." That last statement explains how the parent sees the world—as a place that has dishes that need to be cleaned—but it doesn't create an obligation on any of her children.

In contrast, saying "Do the dishes" creates an obligation on the child or children to whom the parent says it. It changes the world from one in which they weren't obligated to one in which they are. What the parent says has an effect on the world. The words themselves perform something. Words can do things as well as describe things. My friends' and my use of the term *performative* derives from this philosophical observation about one of the things language can do. The word *performative* says that the kind of theology we have in mind brings about something in the act of doing theology.

The etymology of the word *theology* suggests that the word means either "talk or reason [*logos*] that is God's" or "talk about God." If we take that etymology seriously, then those doing performative theology take the word *theology* to mean "what God says to us" more than "what the prophets have to say about him," though obviously the two are closely related. A number of scriptures, particularly in 3 Nephi, tell us that God relates to us through an invitation, the invitation to come to him (see, e.g., Isaiah 55:3; Matthew 11:28; John 7:37; 2 Nephi 26:25; 28:32; Alma 5:16; 3 Nephi 9:14; 12:3; 18:25; 21:6; 27:20; 30:2; Mormon 3:2; Moroni 7:34; Doctrine and Covenants 19:41; 45:5). His invitation is real and scripture can make it real for those who read it. A performative theology, therefore, would be one in which God's invitation is enacted in doing theology. Aspirationally, the work of performative theology is to enact the reality of God's love in its readings of scripture.

COME TO CHRIST

For performative theology, what God says in scripture is less a matter of explanation than it is of experience, the experience of invitation: "Come to Christ." Of course, no one would deny that the scriptures invite us to Christ. That seems obvious, perhaps even trite. But those of us doing performative theology believe that the usual ways we read and think about scripture are actually impediments to the scriptures making that invitation: our bad habits make it difficult for the scriptures to speak to us.

Like the hopeful waiting of the so-called prodigal son's father, the invitation to come to Christ is an expression of his love, an invitation to receive that love—whatever words he says as he kisses his son's neck, the father welcomes the son into his love; what the father does, including what he says, enacts

> In the end, close reading should reveal the divine love enacted in scripture.

that love, making it real. Presumably the young man's life was changed by his father's welcome, including whatever he said when he welcomed him. Similarly, the way we live our lives is enriched, made deeper and more meaningful, when we hear God's welcome in scripture. But—like the young man who has taken his inheritance too early and spent it frivolously—sometimes we have difficulty hearing our Father's invitation.

Learning to hear that loving invitation in prophetic language means learning to think in terms of invitation and response more than in terms of explaining propositions. When we read scripture, our reading should recognize the reality of the invitation that scripture enacts through the things it says. If our reading does that, then it will unavoidably also enact our response, positive or negative. The point of performative theology is to read the scriptures in a way that shows their invitational character. Love received and love revealed is at the heart of performative theology.

THE HOW OF SCRIPTURE

But performative theology isn't easy. We come to the things we read already having an idea of what they have to say. In some cases, we have more of an idea than in others, but with scripture we almost always have already been taught or come to conclusions, especially if we have been reading them a long time. The things we have already learned become what we supposedly read when we read the words on the page. And we focus on the facts of scripture more than the invitation that inheres in those facts.

It is as if we see through the words on the page to what we already have learned them to mean, but we don't really read the words themselves. We read our own thoughts and minds rather than the scriptures. The result is that we don't *hear* their invitation to come to Christ as it applies to each of us here and now in the particular way that *this* scripture we are reading makes that invitation (as opposed to the way that other scriptures do), so we also don't demonstrate that hearing in our interpretations. We cannot help but simply repeat ourselves over and over. We cannot help but find the scriptures boring even if we are embarrassed to admit it.

> Performative theology assumes that the language used by the prophets is significant, more significant than the concepts they employ.

I read 1 Nephi 1 and I already supposedly know what it is about. I don't know how many times I've read the story, but the number is large. I know it: Nephi has an education by good parents; Lehi has a dream of the Savior and the Twelve; he preaches to Jerusalem and they rebuff him; Nephi intends to show us the tender mercies of the Lord.

Of course, those things are all true; that is a reasonable synopsis of the first chapter of the Book of Mormon. But why does Nephi take slightly more than one thousand words to say what I have just written in fewer than forty? Yes, my forty words need expansion to tell the whole story. I've just listed topics, and those topics could be expanded. In spite of that, even if I expand my topics the facts of the story can be told in considerably fewer than one thousand words. There must be some point to not only the facts of what Nephi says but *how* he says them and how they compare with other things that prophets have said.

In 1 Nephi 1:5 we might notice that, curiously, Nephi says that his father, Lehi, was praying *as* he went forth and ask ourselves, "Why does Nephi put it that way?" Thinking about that question, Adam Miller responded this way:

> [T]he layering of action conveys a sense of urgency. It gives the impression that there's no time for Lehi to stop and pray. Even while he is going forth, he is already praying. . . . On Nephi's account, Lehi's "going forth" is explicitly linked to his hearing the call to repent. "There came many prophets prophesying unto the people that they must repent," Nephi says, "*wherefore* . . . my father Lehi, as he went forth, prayed." This *wherefore* implies a direct connection between Lehi's hearing the call to repent and his going forth. And more, by way of additional confirmation, we're told that as he's going forth Lehi is already pleading on behalf of his people. Lehi, it seems safe to say, is going out to pray and repent. He's going somewhere to plead for forgiveness. And for Lehi, the ritual procedure for doing so would be clear. The protocol for his time and place is that, in

order to repent, he needs to offer sacrifice. Lehi needs to make a burnt offering.[10]

But, Miller notes, instead of going where we might expect Lehi to go to offer his burnt offerings, the Jerusalem Temple, he goes someplace else. Miller wonders why, and beginning from that small detail he begins to look at many other details and develops a careful argument for his conclusion: "To understand the mysteries of God is to understand how it is possible to see many afflictions *and* still be highly favored. This is the mystery: God's redemption does not involve an elimination of all suffering but a transformation of our relationship to that suffering such that the suffering itself becomes a condition of knowledge and favor."[11]

Reading the same chapter, Miranda Wilcox focuses on the familiar phrase from 1 Nephi 1:20, "tender mercies," and wonders how it is connected to the same phrase in the King James translation of the Bible, with particular interest in Psalm 25:6.[12] Then, paying careful attention to the Hebrew behind the phrase, she asks how it creates a frame for Nephi's account of his father's experience in Jerusalem and concludes:

> In the first chapter of Nephi's record, he introduces his theological project to produce a record that reveals and testifies of a particular form of divine-human relations characterized by "tender mercies," in which suffering affliction and knowing God are interlinked. In narrating his father's story, Nephi illustrates

---

10. Adam S. Miller, "Burnt Offerings: Favor, Afflictions, and the Mysteries of God," in *A Dream, a Rock, and a Pillar of Fire: Reading 1 Nephi 1*, ed. Adam S. Miller (Provo, UT: Neal A. Maxwell Institute for Religious Scholarship, 2017), 18.

11. Miller, "Burnt Offerings," 29.

12. Miranda Wilcox, "Tender Mercies in English Scriptural Idiom and in Nephi's Record," in Miller, *A Dream, a Rock, and a Pillar of Fire*.

how humans invite divine beings to participate in their mortal experiences and how divine beings invite humans to participate in the sacred story of salvation.[13]

> Prayerful close reading can make seemingly old things new again, giving us new insight into scriptures that we thought we knew thoroughly.

Both Wilcox and Miller give their interpretations of 1 Nephi to help others see the text anew, to read it as something fresh. Of course, they read it as teaching correct principles. But they also use specific points about the details of the text to help us hear the invitation(s) of the text again, and scripture suggests that hearing that invitation is more important than learning the principles.

Many will be surprised to learn that, with others, these two readers spent most of the day for two weeks in a seminar reading and talking about 1 Nephi 1—and the group didn't run out of details to talk about or come to a point where they had no more insights. As early as the second day of the seminar, the participants realized that they were going to have a difficult time getting through even the few verses assigned for each day, and that realization continued through the last day of the two weeks. All of the participants in the seminar had read 1 Nephi 1 many times. But when they focused on the details of the scriptural passage and asked what those details might show us, they discovered that the chapter that had been, perhaps, too familiar, so familiar that there seemed to be nothing left to be said of it, was filled with new insight.

We are admonished to read the scriptures again and again. But if there is only one meaning to them, some set of facts about

13. Wilcox, "Tender Mercies," 106.

things that we are supposed to learn—if the point is to finally reveal the one probably metaphysical meaning to which scripture supposedly points—then it would seem that we would get closer and closer to that one truth of the One as we read scripture over and over. But as the 1 Nephi 1 seminar participants experienced— and I think the experience of many other Latter-day Saints echoes that of those in the seminar—that isn't what happens.

We learn more because we see and experience more, but we don't get closer to the end of new learning. If anything, the more we read carefully, the more we learn and the more we understand that much remains to be learned. When we read attentively, our experience is that the scriptures reveal different things at different times to different people. One reason is because we have different questions or are in different life situations. But if we are doing performative theology, looking for what the scriptures are doing by what they say, another reason is especially because we focus on different details than we did the last time we read them.

In the terms I've been using, scripture reveals the depth of the Many rather than the finality of the One. In one sense, we could perhaps say that there is only one meaning to scripture: "Come unto Christ." But there is no one fact about what that means. We know that the point of scripture is to bring us to Christ, but as Lacoste reminded us, the facts by themselves won't do that, even if they were to be theoretically sound. As Kierkegaard says, Christianity demands that we live it, not that we understand it. The martyrs for Judaism and Christianity and the Restoration did not die for facts. They died as a way of expressing what it means to live as a follower of Jesus Christ. The point of reading scripture is to learn to live differently, and that learning is not something we do one day and then need not continue. It is something we must continue to do for a lifetime. We are given scripture to help us live differently, more than to help us know more.

CONCLUSION

Of course, the close reading of performative theology cannot guarantee that it will bring us to Christ by itself. No method of reading or interpreting can give such a guarantee because so much depends on our willingness to hear and things like the disposition we bring to our study and even the quotidian things that may distract us. But whereas looking for the facts imitates science's methods—deciding what truths are factual and relating them to each other and to some historical situation or set of objects—the point of close reading is not to ascertain what the facts are but to begin with the scriptures as "the word of the Lord" (Doctrine and Covenants 84:45) and to discover what that word is.

The facts are likely to be useful, but they are not themselves the point. The point is to *hear* the word of God. On that basis, performative theology should invite readers into relationship with Christ through reading prophetic writing. It should help others see how the scriptures make their invitation—how they perform it—by performing the invitation in writing about scripture.

> Performative theology aims to show the invitation to the love of God that is enacted in scripture by using attention to the details of prophetic language to help us think anew about what the scriptures say.

As you will see in the next two chapters, close readers don't consciously begin with a theory of what the scriptures say. Instead, they pay attention to such things as the order of the facts or Nephi's word choice, the things he omits, what he says little about and what he focuses on, the implicit comparisons he makes to other scripture. Attention to such details isn't the point of close reading. The reason for paying attention to details is that they can help break us out of our habits of reading, interrupting what we think we already know.

Reading the details, a person makes herself open to the questions that arise as she gives her attention to the details of what is written and uses her imagination to give a faithful account of the text in response to those questions. She must be faithful to the text; this is not an excuse for making whatever she wants of what she reads. What she reads is not a Rorschach ink blot. The question is not what she thinks but what it reveals. The facts are data for revelation but not the revelation itself. The interpreter's job is to allow the revelatory invitation to show itself.

We do performative theology to help us get beyond merely the facts so that we can see—and show—which features of the text tend to invite us to the love of God that is shed abroad in our hearts (see 1 Nephi 11:22), the love manifest in his Son, Jesus Christ. To do that we must imitate his love. Doing performative theology, we must invite others to hear that love by what we say of it as we read carefully.

CHAPTER FIVE

Doing Performative Theology

IT'S ALL IN THE DETAILS

Two questions follow from what I've said so far: What does performative theology look like, and how do you do it? There's a sense in which the second question is either easier to answer than the first or much harder. It could be much harder because there's no one technique for studying scripture. As I said, there can be no method that guarantees that my reading will be revelatory. But it isn't difficult to give an overview of what the close reading of performative theology entails.

First, performative theology values the question over the statement.

To do close reading, a person must ask what questions are raised by the text he or she is reading. Perhaps all of our questions can be divided into two groups, those that ask something of us and those that we ask. The latter are important, but from a theological point of view the former are even more important—questions such as, Do you live in a just, in other words righteous, society? What is the believer's responsibility when society is unjust? What is it like to live a faithful life? What does keeping covenant with God require? Keeping covenant with fellow believers? With family?

Of course, eventually any theology has to result in statements of what its author understands the truth to be, truths that give one a way of connecting the aspects of the world into a whole. But such statements come as responses to questions, and those questions are likely to last longer than our responses to them; we may find ourselves returning to the same questions over and over again and being reinvigorated by considering them.

Sometimes we come at those larger questions because a particularity in a passage of scripture catches our attention. Reading Mosiah 4, I might be struck by the question, What does King Benjamin mean by *beggar*? And that might lead me to ask about my own justice toward the beggar as well as that of my community. However I respond to it, the question about that particular detail of King Benjamin's sermon will probably remain. Questions are starting points. Surely they will lead to insights and claims, but the same questions will not always lead to the same insights or claims.

Perhaps all theology begins something like that, responding to questions that occur as one reads. The difference between other theologies and performative theology is that performative theology depends on a different connection between the particular features of scripture, questions about the details of the text, and the larger questions that scripture asks us. In contrast to a theology that begins with a general question and then asks how scripture can answer that question (and thereby runs the danger of merely proof-texting), performative theology begins with the questions about textual details, with the inquirer hoping that the larger questions and their answers will arise from them.

Second, performative theology begins with questions about the details of the text, such as:

- Why this word rather than that word?
- Where else do we see the word or phrase used?
- How is this word use related to other uses?
- Would it make sense to punctuate the verse differently, and how would doing so change the meaning?
- Are there multiple meanings for a given word, and how does each of the different meanings change the meaning of the whole?
- What is the effect of the various kinds of repetition in our verse or verses?
- Does something appear to have been omitted, and if so, so what?
- Are there places where the grammar is incomplete, where, for example, the writer or speaker seems to have begun a thought, interrupted it, and then moved on to a new thought? What does that suggest?
- How is the section of verses I am studying related to what comes immediately before and after it?
- Does the chapter division (usually not a feature of the original scripture) separate things that properly belong together?
- How does this version of a particular scriptural story or sermon compare to a similar one? How, for example, do the various stories of the Creation (Genesis, Moses, and Abraham) compare to one another, and what do their differences suggest?
- How did prophets who lived before the writing I am studying use the same words and phrases? How is their use the same? How is it different? How might those earlier uses have influenced the use in this text?
- How have prophets since those words or phrases were first written used them to teach? What are the similarities and

differences in use or meaning between scriptural usage and that of contemporary prophets?

These and similar questions about the text are the starting points for a performative theological work. But they are only starting points—and they can also be starting points for completely humdrum, picayune, and spiritually stultifying ways of avoiding scripture's invitation. The questions that the text we are reading raises are important only to the degree that they make us think, we hope, in new ways. Questions like these can do that only if the point of asking them is to break us loose from the habits we've developed for interpreting scripture without hearing what it does.

SCRIPTURE AS PERFORMATIVE

Performative theology understands the scriptures as performative, as doing things, accomplishing something beyond telling stories, listing laws, or giving descriptions. It understands scripture as creating a different world for those who hear it and calling them to inhabit that world. The books of scripture can be put in many genres—law, poetry, rebuke, call to repentance, history, and so on. But *scripture* isn't another genre. Instead, the word *scripture* describes writings of various genres that, over time, Christians have agreed do something for us: they reveal the love of God in some particular way; they call us from a world in which that love is not obvious into one in which it is.

Performative theology assumes that if the scriptures are performative, then the best theology will show their performative character. Performative theology intends not just to talk about the love of God as if the writer were an observer describing what she sees, but to help others see the invitation of God's love by reading scripture in a way that extends its invitation to the theologian's readers.

That doesn't mean that performative theology is warm and fuzzy. God's love is not always warm, nor is his love always the explicit theme of what he says. A call to repentance, for example, may not explicitly mention God's love, but it is a manifestation of it. And whatever the emotional tone of God's love, performative theology isn't about emotions. If it were, it would be about the person writing or her audience rather than about the scriptures and what they reveal.

A writer telling us about the emotional impact of scripture says, "This is how these verses affect me" rather than "This is what these verses allow us to see and hear that we don't see without revelation." In contrast to the person telling how scripture affects her, performative theology wants us to hear how the scriptures perform God's love and how that love invites us to have faith, to repent, to come to Christ, and to endure to the end—however we feel about that invitation. Performative theology wants us to hear the invitation, whether we accept or reject it.

But performative theology ought to not only help us see that the scriptures enact God's invitation to his love. Someone doing performative theology ought herself to enact that invitation in the way that she responds to the details of the text and the questions raised by those details. In the end, performative theology is a goal more than a method or something one can claim to have done. It is the goal of showing what one knows because one loves what has been discovered, namely the love of Christ. To do performative theology is to show the love one has found by helping others see how scripture invites us to the love of Christ.

That brings us back to the initial question, What does performative theology look like? With considerable temerity, I offer two examples from my own work: in this chapter, a reading of Moses

5:1–12;[1] in the next chapter, a reading of Doctrine and Covenants 121. The questions that drive my analyses are not always obvious, though I hope it isn't difficult for readers to see them behind what I've written. Readers will have to judge for themselves how successful my approaches are at inviting them to repent and come to Christ—in other words, to answer the call of scripture by helping them see the text afresh.

> The goal of performative theology is to enact the scriptural invitation to partake of the love of God.

A FIRST EXAMPLE: COVENANT MERCY AND THE HOLY GHOST (MOSES 5:1–12)

MOSES VERSUS GENESIS

The beginning of Moses 5 interrupts a story that is otherwise similar to the Genesis account. It inserts another story and rewrites some of what we find in Genesis. The Book of Moses puts its new story between the expulsion from the Garden of Eden and the birth of Cain (see Moses 5:1–16). Part of what Moses inserts (vv. 1–3) and the first part of verse 16 are an introduction to the story of Cain and Abel. But the introduction is itself interrupted by a reflection on prayer, obedience, and sacrifice (vv. 4–9); a reflection on the positive consequences of Adam and Eve's transgression (vv. 10–12); and a brief homily on the need to repent (vv. 13–15).

---

1. An earlier version of this essay was published as James E. Faulconer, "The Way toward the Garden: Moses 5:1–12," in *Perspectives on Mormon Theology: Scriptural Theology*, ed. James E. Faulconer and Joseph M. Spencer (Salt Lake City: Kofford Books, 2015), 181–93.

The authority of these interruptions is underscored by the fact that they are told to us by the voice of "I, the Lord God" (Moses 5:1) rather than by the anonymous and perhaps human narrator or redactor of Genesis. This is not a story told by a human being, not even if that human being is Moses. It is God's story, and Moses is his amanuensis.

The most obvious interpretation of the Genesis version of the Adam and Eve story is that we move from the expulsion in Genesis 3 to the beginning of human community in Genesis 4:1 with the beginning of the family, specifically with the birth and naming of the first person to enter into that family: Cain. Other children, and their work, follow that birth. In contrast, in the Book of Moses, we move from the expulsion to human labor and *then* to the family, with multiple sons and daughters mentioned before any of them are named.

The story of the beginning of Adam and Eve's mortality in Genesis and in Moses significantly differ. Rather than assuming that one is correct and the other is incorrect, we can learn something by comparing them.

CHRONOLOGY?

The account in Moses immediately creates an interpretive problem: we are told in verse 2 that Adam and Eve have sons and daughters, but Cain—though traditionally the first human born—is not mentioned until verse 16. According to the Book of Moses, is or is not Cain the first child born to Adam and Eve?

There are two possible ways to understand this passage in answer to that question: We can read it as a simple chronology: Adam and Eve have children who also have children and then later, after they learn about sacrifice and come to realize the effects of their transgression in the Garden, Adam and Eve have Cain and Abel.

Or we can understand Moses 5 to begin with a general statement about Adam and Eve and their children (vv. 1–3); to stop to digress on sacrifice, obedience, and repentance (vv. 4–15); and then to return in verse 16 to the specifics of the story of the first family by telling of the births of the first two children, Cain and Abel (vv. 16–17).

I prefer the second of these readings because it creates more harmony between the Genesis and the Moses texts, though choosing one reading over the other doesn't result in significant contradictions between the two. But as I will try to show, focusing on the second way of understanding the story enlarges what it may mean.

LABOR AND FAMILY

The first three verses of Moses 5 give us an explicit theme that is, at best, implicit in Genesis, namely, the inseparability of labor and family. In both Moses 4 and Genesis 3, Adam is told that because he has done what Eve asked him to do—eaten of the fruit of the tree of knowledge—he must labor. Eve is told that because she has eaten of the fruit of the tree, she will endure the pain of childbirth.

But both of these are spoken of as consequences rather than punishments. The verses in question never speak of punishment. The serpent is explicitly said to be cursed, but not Adam and Eve. Labor and childbirth result from what has happened, but we need not believe they are punishments.

Even in Genesis these two results are not as different as we might think. That we use the term *labor* to denote childbirth in English is helpful. Coincidentally, the Hebrew words for work and childbirth are also closely related. That coincidence, however, helps us see something: both labor and childbirth require work. Both involve pain. Both create.

Central to each act is the fact that human beings are in relationships with one another. That this is true of childbirth is obvious. But it is also true of labor. To labor is labor for more than myself. If I produce something by my labor, I produce it for the use of others. If I work in a service industry, I work to serve others in some way. No one is Robinson Crusoe. Work is a human, relational activity.

The Moses account makes the intertwining of labor and childbirth explicit at the beginning of chapter 5:

Verse 1: Adam and Eve labor together.
Verse 2: Adam and Eve have children; their children have
children.
Verse 3: Their children labor and bear children, imitating
their parents.

Verse 3 brings the themes of the first two verses together as one: to be a child of Adam and Eve is to labor and bear children. The two are inseparable from each other. Labor and childbirth, the supposed curses of Adam and Eve, are not separable and distinct duties but two aspects of one thing, the fullness of human life.

CALLING ON GOD

But, as verse 4 shows us, labor and family are not yet enough for full life, for Adam and Eve also call on God. The Book of Moses account directly disagrees with Genesis here. For though Moses suggests that Adam and Eve "called upon the name of the Lord" as part of the intertwining of labor and family that begins immediately after the expulsion, we don't see that phrase until much later in the Genesis story, not in fact until Genesis

4:26: "And to Seth . . . also there was born a son; and he called his name Enos: *then*[2] began men to call upon the name of the Lord" (emphasis added). In Genesis, only in the third generation does anyone explicitly call on the name of the Lord. In contrast, in Moses, Adam and Eve know and call on his name from the beginning. That makes calling on his name more obvious as a theme in Moses.

But what does it mean to say that Adam and Eve call on God? The text specifically says that they call "upon the *name* of the Lord" (emphasis added). He isn't an impersonal force or someone unknown. He may not be present, but he is not anonymous. Adam and Eve call on someone they know, and using his name their prayers have the force that the petitions of someone we know would have on us. Their use of his name suggests a covenant relation between him and them, whether formal or not, a relation of obligation and service like the obligation of children to a father and vice-versa. The whole point of a covenant, after all, is to make it possible for the covenanted parties to call on each other, to recognize their mutual obligations.

Adam and Eve's prayer is not only prayer. In most Genesis texts the formula "call on the name of the Lord" suggests prayer and sacrifice. Indeed, if we pay close attention to the use of that formula in Genesis, we see that it most often appears to imply covenant, ritual worship (see, e.g., Genesis 12:8; 13:4; 21:33; 26:25). For Adam and Eve life in the world includes not just prayer but ritual worship. Human life begins in work, family, and the covenant relation with God that ritual expresses and makes real. We do not see ritual yet. It comes later in the story. But its necessity is suggested early on.

In Moses, Adam and Eve *call* on God because he is not present to them. They must call on him because they are outside the

---

2. The Hebrew is *ʾāz* (אָז), "at that time."

Garden of Eden. They have been "shut out from his presence" (Moses 5:4). It is significant that the human life of work and family—fullness of life—comes about not in God's presence but in his absence. To be in the mortal world of labor and family is to be separated from the Father.

But as is obvious in the story, "shut out from his presence" and "cut off" do not mean the same. After the expulsion, Adam and Eve continue to hear the Lord speaking "from the way toward the Garden of Eden" (Moses 5:4). They have not been abandoned, though the Lord is not directly present to them.

THE WAY OF NOSTALGIA

Considering the distance between the place in the world where Adam and Eve find themselves and the Garden, notice an interesting phrase in verse 4: "Adam and Eve . . . heard the voice of the Lord from the way toward the Garden of Eden." There is a way, a path, leading toward the Garden. Without multiple trips from Adam and Eve's home to the Garden's entrance, trips enough to wear a path, could there be such a way? I doubt it. And what would be the point of these trips toward the gate of the Garden? Obviously every path goes both to and from its end points, but the text emphasizes that this way goes *toward* the Garden. The way is described from the point of view of someone not yet at the Garden.

> In mortality, Adam and Eve are not cut off from God. Though separated from him, they continue to be in covenant relationship with him through prayer and sacrifice.

I imagine the first couple treading their way toward the garden gate, hoping for contact with the Lord and being disappointed until they return home and hear that voice from afar (as we hear his voice from afar through the scriptures and the words of the prophets). I imagine them hoping that even if they are not to be readmitted to the Garden of Eden, then perhaps by returning to its edge they will once again be brought into at least the nimbus of God's presence.

But the journey on which this way leads them—presumably many times—is a disappointment. The only presence they find there is perhaps the fearful presence of the cherubim with their flaming sword (see Moses 4:31; Genesis 3:24). Adam and Eve have made a path to the Garden looking for what they can have only at home, though what they receive at home is not quite what they went looking for at the Garden. It is a voice from afar rather than an immediate presence. As I read verse 4, the path Adam Eve have trodden toward the Garden of Eden suggests that they are nostalgic for that garden.

Nostalgia is a common experience. Perhaps I should be embarrassed to admit it, but the older I grow, the more often I experience nostalgia. A mission reunion makes me nostalgic for the time I spent as a missionary. A message on Facebook from a high school friend makes me nostalgic for my adolescence. The visit of grandchildren makes me nostalgic for their halcyon infancy and for the childhood of my now-grown children, as well as my own childhood.

> **Perhaps Adam and Eve's first response to their expulsion from the Garden is nostalgia, longing for a lost past.**

Nostalgia is a kind of yearning, and yearning is an emotion that may be uniquely human, perhaps the most inclusive form of human desire. Adam and Eve's nostalgia for the Garden shows that they are fully human.

But nostalgia never yearns for what really was. There was much about my mission that was wonderful, but it was also difficult, sufficiently difficult that I would not want to do it again. High school was, in fact, awful, vexed by teenage hormones and adolescent worries, driven by a brain not yet developed enough to make well-grounded moral decisions but making decisions anyway. I very much prefer being older, thank you.

And as much as I love my grandchildren, the times for which I am nostalgic are chosen selectively from a much wider canvas on which the pastel colors of babies and loving four-year-olds are mixed with the more dramatic colors of full-blooded, real, "nonhalcyon," developing children. As nostalgia, yearning is a pleasant-feeling form of self-pity for the passage of time—and it is a deception.

Adam and Eve's nostalgia for the Garden of Eden takes the outward form of a hope to return to the presence of God in the Garden, but that hope is implicitly also a hope to return to a state of bliss, a state free of difficulty and overflowing with plenty. Nostalgia for the Garden of Eden conflates being in the presence of God with bliss, plenty, and freedom from pain.

In spite of scriptural and prophetic evidence to the contrary, our dreams of heaven are often formed from such nostalgia: we dream that in heaven there is no pain and that there is no labor. Unfortunately, in such a heaven there would probably also be neither personal relationship nor even personal identity. For the nostalgic, heaven is nothing but continual bliss and, so, probably nothing at all.

I suspect those nostalgic, Edenic dreams of the heavenly garden to come also inform our hope for the possibilities of mortality. When we think about family or communal life, we often do so in nostalgic terms, hoping not only that the earth will be "renewed and receive its paradisiacal glory" (Articles of Faith 1:10), but that our earthly lives will approach those of Adam and Eve in the Garden of Eden. The problem with such hope is that the promised heavenly paradise and the Garden of Eden are not the same.

In the Garden of Eden, Adam and Eve were not yet fully human. Their eyes were as yet unopened; they were not only blissful but ignorant. Indeed, perhaps there is no bliss without ignorance. Nostalgic dreaming that fullness of life means bliss amounts to dreaming that we can escape our humanity rather than fulfill that humanity in labor and family. We cannot undo the fact that, as the children of Adam and Eve, we too have eaten of the fruit of the tree of the knowledge of good and evil. Our eyes are open and, at least in principle, we are as the Gods (see Moses 4:28) and cannot return to the childhood of Eden.

Nostalgia for an assumed Edenic life, in which there is neither toil nor pain, is a deceptive desire for life that is not human, life without the knowledge of good and evil. Implicitly, such nostalgia is a desire that we no longer have the potential to be like God.

THE VOICE OF THE LORD

Nostalgia for something like an Eden conceals from us the truth of what it means to have the divine knowledge of good and evil, presumably an ongoing knowledge rather than something true of this life only. But the divine knowledge of good and evil is necessarily also the knowledge of work, pain, loss—and joy. As the Father and Son can personally testify, heaven is not simply bliss. Indeed, it isn't bliss, though it is the fullness of the possibility of joy.

It is pointless to go back and forth to the Garden. Our first parents will find nothing at its end that they don't already have without treading that path. All they can have at the gate of the Garden is the voice of the Lord, but they can hear the voice of the Lord speaking to them from where they are without going back. His voice comes when they call on him, and verse 4 may imply that they call only after they've trodden the way to the Garden, after whatever time it would take to make that path. Perhaps our first parents call on the Lord in prayer only after they've given up their nostalgia.

In any case, like them we learn that nostalgia for bliss—in other words, nostalgia for ignorance—will give us nothing. We, too, stand some distance outside the presence of God, where we, too, can hear the voice of the Lord, in spite of his absence. And we hear that voice, not at the gate of the Garden of Eden, but where we are within the world of labor and family: labor by the sweat of our brows, the labor of and for families, the labor of Adam and Eve working together, of Adam and Eve multiplying and replenishing the earth together. That is where we find the knowledge of good and evil. In that work, we can already become as the Gods *here in the world*, where we can hear the voice of the Lord even when outside his face-to-face presence.

The Lord responds to Adam and Eve's call, commanding them to worship and sacrifice (see Moses 5:5). In answer to Adam and Eve's longing to be in his presence, he continues to remain absent, but never absolutely absent. In particular, he is present to them in the command to sacrifice the firstlings of their flocks. The Lord's answer to their call is to not only reject their nostalgia for his presence and the garden, but to ask them to forfeit the first part of their present plenty.

SACRIFICE

In the world, human fullness requires labor, the labor to produce what we need to live, a need that tends toward the desire for fullness and plenty and excess. But the Lord's command interrupts that tendency of desire to suggest that human fullness is not the same as a fullness of material needs. For the command requires sacrificing those material needs, giving some of them up, in order to live fully.

Surely Adam found this answer to his prayers puzzling: he calls on the Lord, asking, as it were, "Lord be with me," and the Lord answers, saying what amounts to "Worship me and offer sacrifice." Puzzled or not, as every Latter-day Saint knows, Adam obeys, trusting that God will be with him in that ritual. As Moses 5:6 tells us, Adam does not know why he is sacrificing from his flocks, but he understands that sacrifice is more than just giving something up. More importantly, it is also *sacri-fying*, making sacred. Sacrificing the firstborn of his flocks shows that Adam understands that his flocks are sacred, not his property but that of the Lord. I assume that "worship and sacrifice" belong together in the same way that "labor and childbirth" do. Each word in the pair says the same thing; the phrase is said to be a hendiadys, two words expressing the same meaning. In worship, sacrifice brings us into God's presence, though it is not obvious to Adam at this point how or why that is so.

In the next part of the story, though the temporal distance is great ("many days," v. 6), the spatial distance between Adam and the Garden of Eden apparently remains the same. But he no longer needs to tread the way across that distance. Now engaged in worship and sacrifice, Adam is no longer nostalgic. He has given up his yearning for presence and plenty. He lives in the world of his humanity without seeking to leave it for an inhuman, prehuman realm. Nostalgia has been replaced by obedience: "Why dost thou offer sacrifices?" an angel asks. "I know not, save the Lord commanded me," answers Adam (v. 6).

Sometimes when we talk about this story we say that Adam doesn't know why he offers sacrifice, but that isn't quite right. He doesn't merely say, "I know not." He says, "I know not, save the Lord commanded me." In other words, "I know only one reason, that I was commanded to do so."

Adam makes the sacrifice because in it the relationship he has with the Lord happens: the desire to be in the presence of the Lord in the Garden is taken up into and changed into something new: presence in religious rite, an event that brings one into relation with Another. Ritual worship in response to the voice of the Lord has taken the place of nostalgia for presence because it brings us before God. We have many such rituals in the Church today—ordinances and rites such as baptism, confirmation, the blessing of babies, settings apart, the sacrament, blessings of healing and comfort, our temple rites. Though at first glance the worship of members of The Church of Jesus Christ of Latter-day Saints would appear to be informal, almost devoid of ritual, a closer look shows that ritual is very much part of our worship. Along with personal prayer, perhaps the most important way that we find ourselves in God's presence is through rites and ordinances.

Yet Adam does not yet know why the Lord has commanded the particular rite of animal sacrifice. We could understand the angel's question to amount to "Why does your covenant with the Lord require the sacrifice of

Adam and Eve return to the presence of God through ritual worship—ordinance—rather than by returning to the Garden.

your firstlings?" To that question, Adam's answer would be a simple "I don't know."

IN SIMILITUDE AND COVENANT MERCY

What happens in the covenant of ritual worship is only implicit until the angel makes it explicit by telling Adam that sacrificial worship is a similitude of the sacrifice of the Only Begotten of the Father (see Moses 5:7). Webster's 1828 *American Dictionary of the English Language* reflects American English usage at the time of Joseph Smith. It gives "likeness" and "resemblance" as definitions for *similitude*: what Adam performs in sacrifice is a likeness of what the Only Begotten will do.

Compare *similitude* here with *likeness* in the King James Bible, for example in Deuteronomy 5:8: "Thou shalt not make thee any graven image, or any likeness of any thing that is in heaven above, or that is in the earth beneath, or that is in the waters beneath the earth." *Likeness* translates the Hebrew word *temuna*, clearly meaning something like "form."

If the word *similitude* in Moses 5:7 has the same meaning as *likeness* in Deuteronomy 5:8, then covenant, ritual worship enacts the presence of God for Adam: the act of sacrifice is in the form of the sacrifice that the Messiah, he who is full of grace and truth, will make. The elevation toward God that comes through worship is informed and made possible by Jesus's life and condescension. Though Jesus is full of grace and truth and therefore doesn't need to offer sacrifice, he does so anyway, precisely because he is full of grace—of giving—and of truth—of right relation to the Father. Adam's act is an enactment, a similitude brought about in what one does, of that gracious gift.

The angel's description of the Only Begotten as "full of grace and truth" (Moses 5:7) repeats a phrase that we are familiar with from John 1:14: "And the Word was made flesh, and dwelt among us, (and we beheld his glory, the glory as of the only begotten of the Father,) full of grace and truth." At first glance we might assume that this is an anachronism imported into the Book of Moses translation through Joseph Smith's familiarity with the New Testament. But the Johannine phrase appears to be a repetition of the Hebrew formula *hesed we emeth*, most often translated as "mercy and truth" (e.g., 2 Samuel 15:20), but also translated as "lovingkindness and truth" (Psalm 40:10–11), "goodness and truth" (e.g., Exodus 34:6), or, of course, "grace and truth," as in John 1:14.

In the Hebrew Bible, the phrase describes God's covenant mercy, which is why John uses a translation of that language to describe his experience of the Son. John is using the same phrase he finds in the writings of his scriptures, something very close to our Old Testament. Presumably the Book of Moses uses John's language for the same reason that he uses the language of the Hebrew Bible, though he wrote in Greek. It appears that both are repeating the same ancient, meaningful phrase, though in different languages. The self-revelation of the Only Begotten as merciful, loving, and full of truth is present to Adam and his family in the ritual of sacrifice.

The covenant enacted in sacrifice is a covenant of mercy, mercy that has two aspects. It is, of course, God's promise of mercy to those who will be his people. It is also a demand for his people's mercy to others. That is their imitation or enactment of his mercy and, so, their way of being like him. Further, Adam's ritual sacrifice enacts a covenant with the Lord because it has the same form as the divine life of the Only Begotten of the Father, namely sacrifice. Fullness of human life requires sacrifice rather than mere plenty because fullness of divinity requires it. To be God is to own everything and, yet, also to give it all away to those who will receive it: "He that receiveth my Father receiveth my Father's kingdom; therefore all that my Father hath shall be given unto him" (Doctrine and Covenants 84:38).

Just as God's Only Begotten will give up his life, Adam must ritually repeat that sacrifice by giving up a significant token of what sustains his life. In sacrifice Adam memorializes the sacrifice of the Only Begotten, and by doing that he acts out the possibility of his own divinization, of being like the Gods in sacrifice. In covenant, ritual worship Adam and Eve remember who they are by acting out the mercy that joins human beings to the Gods through the condescension of the Son, and they remember that the imitation of that mercy makes it possible for them to be like the Gods.

> Adam's sacrifice, giving up a token of what sustains his life and that of his family, is a likeness of Christ's mercy and his right relation to the Father, an imitation of what it means to be divine.

THE GIFT OF COVENANT

"In that day" (Moses 5:10), rather than after many days, Adam regains what he had sought when he and Eve wore a path to the Garden of Eden. He regains the presence of God. But the presence comes on him, as if by surprise. It is not something he discovers: "The Holy Ghost *fell upon* Adam" (v. 9). Adam doesn't *do* something, he *receives* something. This is not the presence of a mere form. Adam cannot see God, so he remains at a distance from him. At the same time, however, he *is* in the presence of God, an embodied being, in covenant and through ritual worship. It is the same for us: rather than our finding that presence in a well-trodden, nostalgic return to Eden—in ease, bliss, and plenty—the presence of God in covenant falls on us as the Holy Spirit when we enact divine mercy and sacrifice in labor and family.

It is not just an angelic messenger who speaks to Adam. It is the Godhead in their unity. The verse is clear about that, for it specifically says that the Holy Ghost came to Adam, but when he speaks, he speaks in the name of the Son: ". . . saying, I am the Only Begotten of the Father from the beginning" (Moses 5:9). Speaking as the Son, the Holy Spirit teaches Adam that for human beings there is a parallel between falling and redemption: "as thou hast fallen thou mayest be redeemed" (v. 9).

CONCLUSION

With Adam's understanding of covenant worship and redemption, his eyes are finally fully open. Rejoicing he says, "Because of my transgression my eyes are opened" (Moses 5:10). He now knows what he seems to have previously grasped only sketchily, if at all: he understands that his transgression of the bounds of the Garden of Eden has made it possible for him to be like the Gods. Neither divine nor divinely human existence is blissful ignorance. Neither is a lack of want and freedom from pain.

Human existence, with its divine potential, cannot occur within the boundaries of pain-free, blissful Eden, so the desire to return to Eden is implicitly a rejection of human and divine existence. Instead, that existence happens in covenant relation to others in mercy—which requires sacrifice and being in truth. And divinely human existence is existence in *this* world rather than someplace else: "In this life I shall have joy, and again in the flesh I shall see God" (Moses 5:10).

Though one popular Latter-day Saint understanding of the Garden of Eden is that Eve realized the necessity of eating the fruit and made the choice to do so conscious of what that disobedience would mean, the Book of Moses may suggest something else. It isn't until verse 11 that Eve seems to understand the blessing that comes from her and Adam's transgression: "Were it not for our transgression we never should have had seed, and never should have known good and evil, and the joy of our redemption, and the eternal life which God giveth unto all the obedient."

> Adam and Eve learn that to be before God (fullness of life) is to be engaged fully in this world of work and family rather than in some other wished-for world of bliss.

Eve learns what she says in verse 11 only after she and Adam have made their choice to eat from the tree of knowledge *and* after they are cast out. Together with Adam, Eve comes to know that joy is the joy of labor, family, and covenant life, but they learn that lesson in the world, engaged in labor and pain and family, and not before. In this passage from the Book of Moses, Adam and Eve learn that covenant life in the presence of God requires them to be outside the Garden of Eden. It requires labor and pain and regaining the presence of God through continually keeping or regaining the presence of the Holy Ghost, who, as the third member of the Godhead, is also a God.

CHAPTER SIX

A Gentle Rebuke and a Powerful Promise:
Doctrine and Covenants 121

HISTORICAL BACKGROUND

Doctrine and Covenants 121 consists of excerpts from two letters by Joseph Smith sent from the jail in Liberty, Missouri, to Edward Partridge (the Church's first Presiding Bishop). Verses 1 through 33 are from a letter sent on 20 March 1839.[1] The rest of the section, verses 34 through 46, are from a letter sent about two days later.[2]

Much of the two letters is powerful, and though they contain a number of striking passages, not all of them have been canonized. For example, in the first letter Smith writes:

---

1. Joseph Smith, "Letter to the Church and Edward Partridge, 20 March 1839," 3–4, 8–10, 13–15, The Joseph Smith Papers, https://www.josephsmith papers.org/paper-summary/letter-to-the-church-and-edward-partridge -20-march-1839. Hereafter referred to as "20 March Letter."

2. Joseph Smith, "Letter to Edward Partridge and the Church, circa 22 March 1839," pp. 2–3, The Joseph Smith Papers, https://www.josephsmithpapers .org/paper-summary/letter-to-edward-partridge-and-the-church-circa -22-march-1839/2.

A fanciful and flowery and heated imagination beware of because the things of God are of deep import, and time and experience and careful and ponderous and solemn thoughts can only find them out. Thy mind, O man, if thou wilt lead a soul unto salvation, must stretch as high as the utmost heavens, and search into and contemplate the lowest considerations of the darkest abyss, and expand upon the broad considerations of eternal expanse; he must commune with God. How much more dignified and noble are the thoughts of God than the vain imagination of the human heart. None but fools will trifle with the souls of men.[3]

I first read an edited version of that passage in Truman Madsen's *Eternal Man*.[4] I was a convert to the Church of no more than three or four years, and the passage plucked a string in my heart that has not ceased to reverberate more than fifty years later. As I said in the introduction to this book, this passage animates it; reading the passage helps me appreciate the seriousness with which I ought to take the teachings of the Restoration. Yet, as inspirational as it has been for me and others, the passage has not been canonized.

The passage suggests how we ought to study scripture, including the scriptures that ultimately issued from the letter in which we find the passage. It suggests that Doctrine and Covenants 121 is an invitation for us to stretch our minds as high as the utmost heavens from which it speaks and to contemplate the dark abysses that it points out. We can commune with God in studying it by reading carefully and using disciplined rather than flowery imagination to think about the meanings that the

---

3.   Smith, "20 March Letter," 12. Spelling and punctuation modernized, and words originally marked for deletion omitted.
4.   Truman G. Madsen, *Eternal Man* (Salt Lake City, UT: Deseret Book, 1966).

scriptural text may have—not perhaps what we see in it at first glance, but what it shows us on careful analysis.

To do that, I will rely on canonized scripture rather than on the original documents from which section 121 came. Ryan J. Wessel describes how this section came into being:

> Portions of the Liberty letter were first published as Doctrine and Covenants 121–23 in the 1876 edition of the Doctrine and Covenants. The portions were selected by Orson Pratt under the direction of President Brigham Young. The edition of the Doctrine and Covenants containing the sections as they currently read was first sustained as scripture at the October 1880 conference of the Church.[5]

Doctrine and Covenants 121 is, therefore, a text created from Joseph Smith's writings at the direction of Brigham Young, when Young was prophet, and then canonized in a conference of the Church thirty-six years after Smith's death and three years after Young's. Section 121 is not the same as the letters from which it was created. Our focus will be on the canonized scripture rather than on the original letters.

> The canonized scripture known as Doctrine and Covenants 121 is not the sum of the uncanonized parts from which it was created; it is a new thing.

Other historians have written about how section 121 can be more meaningful if we see it in its original context.[6] Of course

---

5. Ryan J. Wessel, "The Textual Context of Doctrine and Covenants 121–23," *Religious Educator* 13, no. 1 (2012): 103.

6. A good example is Dean C. Jesse and John W. Welch, "Revelations in Context: Joseph Smith's Letter from Liberty Jail, March 20, 1839," *BYU Studies* 39, no. 3 (2000): 125–45. Note that the Joseph Smith Papers Project offers

that is true. But not all members of The Church of Jesus Christ of Latter-day Saints are historians, nor do they all have the skills needed for historical research. Nevertheless, we can all ask questions about what Doctrine and Covenants 121 means *as scripture.* My contention is that the question of what section 121 means as scripture is different from the question of what it means as parts extracted from historical documents. Presumably, as scripture the section's meaning is available to every literate person with access to either the English version of the section or a good translation, regardless of his or her knowledge of the section's historical background. To study section 121 as scripture is to take it *as it exists in its present canonized form* in the Doctrine and Covenants and to be taught by it in that form.

However, when we study section 121 as scripture, we must pay heed to Joseph Smith's warning that if we want to know the things of God, we must beware of a fanciful, flowery, or heated subjective imagination. That kind of imagination steers scripture to mean whatever pops into our heads when we read it. If passages of scripture mean whatever we imagine them to mean, we risk turning them into mirrors in which we see only ourselves and our ideas and our emotions. In that case they will not teach us, because they will not challenge us and take us beyond where we already are. We must not trifle with our souls or the souls of those we teach by not taking scripture seriously, by taking it to be no more than a mirror of our own ideas. Our question must not be simply, "What does this scripture mean to me?" but "Are there good grounds for believing that it means what I think it does?"

---

anyone with internet access and English language skills access to the historical documents that were once the domain of only academic historians.

OVERVIEW

I understand Doctrine and Covenants 121 to be, from beginning to end, about power, with arguably one exception (vv. 26–33, God's promise to bless the Saints with knowledge). What is power? Who has it? How does one get it? And what do the answers to those questions add up to? As we will see, as a document about power, the section is also a striking example of God doing—enacting and exemplifying—the very thing he enjoins his prophet and us to do.

The section begins with Joseph Smith's bitter complaint about having been done wrong by those who assumed power over him and the Saints. In response to their violence, Smith wants God to bare his mighty arm to tip the scales of justice back into alignment. Smith wants the same kind of coercive power that is presently directed at him and the Saints to be directed at his enemies.

But rather than vengeance, God's answer through the Prophet is kindness and pure knowledge that greatly enlarge the soul. He comforts Smith, even validating his pain. He says nothing to shame Smith for his anger, but at the same time God begins to place matters in a wider context. He doesn't minimize what has happened to Smith and the Saints so much as he puts it in perspective relative to God's grand designs and the sufferings of others: it is possible to be in a much worse position than Joseph Smith currently finds himself in.

Finally, ever so gently, God corrects Smith, helping him to see—and to prophesy—that the power he wants to see wreaked on others is the wrong kind of power. God warns him where the demand for that kind of power will lead, to an "Amen" to personal growth toward godliness. The denouement of the revelation in its last five verses is what one could call "a theology of weakness," culminating with promises of transcendent power, though power that flows effortlessly from having chosen the path of submission, meekness, patience, and godly renunciation (*kenosis* in Philippians 2:7: "made himself of no reputation").

Thus, though the most-often quoted part of section 121 begins in verse 34—"Behold, there are many called, but few are chosen. And why are they not chosen?"—we will first look at the preceding thirty-three verses to help us understand that verse and the answer to its question as well as the beautiful promises of verses 45 and 46.

If we look at the whole of section 121, verses 34 through 46 seem to me to be the last two parts of five into which we can divide the section:

1. Verses 1–6	Joseph Smith's complaint.	
2. Verses 7–25	The voice of the Lord: (1) "Peace to thy soul" and (2) "There is a time appointed for every man, according as his works shall be."	
3. Verses 26–33	Smith responds prophetically: God's promise of divine knowledge.	
4. Verses 34–40	Smith responds reflectively: Why many are called but few are chosen; compulsion and divine power.	
5. Verses 41–46	The voice of the Lord: Persuasion and reproof, and a further promise—confidence before God, the doctrine of the priesthood, the constant companionship of the Holy Ghost, and everlasting dominion	

Divisions of Doctrine and Covenants 121.

Those are the divisions we will use to understand section 121 as a whole, the parts into which we can divide the pieces of Smith's letters that have been stitched together and canonized as scripture. The canonized result looks something like a dialogue:[7] (1) Joseph Smith complains; (2) then the Lord responds with an

---

7.   I am indebted to Morgan Davis for pointing out this dialogic structure.

admonition and a promise that everyone will receive according to their works; (3) Smith responds to the admonition and promise with a prophecy explaining what that promise means for the Saints; (4) then he reflects prophetically on what the Lord has said; and finally (5) the Lord responds approvingly to his reflections.

In section 121, the Lord gently leads Joseph Smith from the desire for vengeance to a "theology of weakness," in which power comes effortlessly and without anger.

THE PROPHET'S COMPLAINT

Joseph Smith's complaint begins: "O God, where are thou? And where is the pavilion that covereth thy hiding place?" (Doctrine and Covenants 121:1). The headnote gives us some historical context for the question: Smith has been in prison for several months and has failed to get judicial relief. The first verses, then, are his desperate cry for relief, and the language he uses gives scriptural context to what he says.

We see here an echo of the ancient literary tradition of complaint and, specifically, the imagery of shelter found in 2 Samuel 22. There David sings a hymn of praise to the Lord for delivering him from his enemies and describes the Lord as surrounded by a pavilion or canopy of darkness (see v. 12).[8] That darkness hides the writer from his enemies. A slight variation of the hymn appears as Psalm 18, and there the Lord is also said to hide in a

---

8. Here, as in the other verses referred to, the word translated "pavilion" is *sūkkâh* or a variation of that word: covering, thicket, booth. Francis Brown, Samuel Rolles Driver, and Charles Augustus Briggs, *Enhanced Brown-Driver-Briggs Hebrew and English Lexicon* (Oxford: Clarendon Press, 1977), 696.

pavilion of darkness (see v. 11). In Psalm 27, another hymn of praise for being saved from enemies, in verse 5 the Lord hides the psalm's author in his pavilion or tent. Similarly, in Psalm 31 the psalmist prays for deliverance from his enemies, saying that the Lord will hide those who fear him from "the strife of tongues" by keeping them "secretly in a pavilion," or hidden shelter (v. 20). Psalm 91:4 uses the verb form of the same Hebrew word to describe the Lord as a fortress offering refuge under the cover of his wings. And Psalm 140:7 uses the verb to say that the Lord covers the psalmist's head in battle. The imagery is the same in each of these: the Lord provides his children with a pavilion of shelter from their enemies, in most cases by hiding them. But Joseph Smith has reversed the imagery, asking in despair where he and the Saints can find that hidden shelter. For him the divine pavilion that ought to hide the Saints from their enemies seems instead to hide the Lord from the Saints.

> In his prophetic lament, Joseph Smith uses Old Testament language praising God for protection, though he reverses the imagery of that language by wondering where the Saints can find the Lord's protection rather than praising him for giving it.

The pathos of the first four verses is unmistakable, coming to a climax in verse 4 with "let thine heart be softened, and thy bowels moved with compassion toward us" and its powerful image of physical experiences we have in moments of intense emotion. "Please, Lord," Smith is begging, "have pity on us." It is not surprising when the next two verses move to a plea for vengeance: don't just take pity on us, but remember us by kindling your anger against our enemies "and, in the fury of thine heart, with thy sword avenge us of our wrongs" (v. 6). Soften your heart toward us, Smith prays, and have fury in your heart toward those who have wronged us; have compassion on us but fierce anger on those who hurt us. In these first four verses, "remember us" means "take vengeance on our enemies." And, if you remember us, Smith promises, we "will rejoice in thy name forever." We will remember you.

To rejoice in something is to take joy in it. It is to find intense satisfaction, happiness, and even pleasure in that thing. I take joy in my grandchildren because they delight me. What Smith says isn't conditional. He isn't making a deal with God; he doesn't say, "We will rejoice in thy name only if you take vengeance on our enemies." Instead he says that if the Lord takes vengeance, the Saints will find happiness and pleasure in his name, presumably in gratitude for their deliverance, for sheltering them from their enemies in his pavilion. They will be unable to forget him. Smith is describing what the result of the Lord's taking vengeance will be rather than making a deal. That said, even if we understand Smith to be saying they will take joy in their gratitude, their joy will still be the result of the suffering of others, something at least ethically problematic if not, in fact, simply wrong.

The first six verses of section 121 set up the general problem to which the section as a whole is a response, "How does one respond to persecution and injustice?" And those verses set up that problem much in the way that people often experience it, as a need for vengeance.

PEACE TO THY SOUL

The Lord's first response to Joseph Smith's complaint on behalf of himself and the Saints is "Peace be unto thy soul" (v. 7).[9]

---

9. In light of my overall reading of Doctrine and Covenants 121, the original context of this phrase is noteworthy:

Whereas the narrative voice has been that of Smith, now it is that of the Lord. What the Lord says here is much like the injunction to be still in Psalm 46:10: "Be still, and know that I am God." That psalm is another hymn about God as a refuge for the Saints, one in which, in response to the wars of the earth, God commands his people to be at peace. Doctrine and Covenants 121:7 seems to echo the psalmic verse. The Hebrew verb translated "be still" in the psalm (*rāpeh*) is not a command like "Shut up." It means "Relax," without the sarcastic connotations that command has for us today. It means "Let go," as in "Let go of your fears and doubts and trust in the Lord." "Be still" and "Peace be unto thy soul" are admonitions to be comforted similar to what we mean when we say to someone in distress, "Don't worry." One reason to think that the injunction to be still is meant to remind us of the psalm is that the entire verse in Psalm 46 is "Be still, and know that I am God: I will be exalted among the heathen, I will be exalted in the earth." In other words, don't worry, for in the end the Lord will triumph and his people with him. That's also God's message to Joseph Smith.

In the psalm, the command to let go of worry and fear is coordinated with the command to know: let go of your fears so that you can know God, who will be exalted. In section 121, hav-

---

Those who have not been enclosed in the walls of a prison without cause or provocation can have but a little idea how sweet the voice of a friend is. One token of friendship from any source whatever awakens and calls into action every sympathetic feeling it brings up. In an instant everything that is passed it [seizes?] the present with a vivacity of lightning. It grasps after the future with the fierceness of a tiger. It retrogrades from one thing to another until finally all enmity, malice, and hatred and past differences, misunderstandings and mismanagements, lie slain victims at the feet of hope, and *when the heart is sufficiently contrite, [then] the voice of inspiration steals along and whispers, "My son, peace be unto thy soul."* (Joseph Smith, "20 March Letter," 7–8; emphasis added and spelling, capitalization, and punctuation standardized)

ing peace is explicitly the prerequisite for Joseph Smith triumphing over his foes (see vv. 7–8): if you succeed in letting go of your fear in adversity, you will be exalted and will triumph. But the difference between the psalm (let go so that you can know) and section 121 (let go so you will be exalted) is less a difference than it might first seem. For what the psalmist will come to know is that God will be exalted—and he is with his people (see Psalm 46:11). In both the psalm and Doctrine and Covenants 121 the same result comes from letting go of one's fear and anger: exaltation, rising to the status of godliness. The balm that God promises Smith is the knowledge—as hope—that God and his people will be exalted in the future, so there is no need to fear in the present.

That balm will be a thread woven through the rest of the section, a powerful theology of fearlessness: To trust in God—and others, such as one's loved ones, insofar as they share that trust in God—allows one the liberty to no longer fear what might have gone wrong in the past or might go wrong in the future. It allows a person to focus instead on what is most real in the sphere that God has granted her. Peace with God banishes fear and brings exaltation.

> The Lord responds to Joseph's plea for vengeance with the admonition to be at peace. Hope for exaltation overcomes fear and brings peace.

With the command to receive peace comes a reminder in verses 9 and 10: you aren't yet like Job, for your friends stand by you. The Lord does not minimize Joseph Smith's suffering or the persecution of the Saints. But he does ask Smith to put that suffering and persecution into perspective. In the end, this imprisonment will have been "but a small moment" (v. 7). Besides that, he and the Saints have each other: "Thy friends do stand by thee, and they shall hail thee again with warm hearts and friendly hands" (v. 9). The image of friendly hands is particularly striking and may have been comforting to Smith. When in pain, it is comforting to have another's hand to hold, to have someone who sits with you in your pain, even if the physical fact of the pain remains the same.

Yet others have suffered completely alone. Worse, in their suffering they were betrayed by their friends and loved ones, people who turned against them and charged them with sin (see v. 10). It may be helpful to know that one's suffering will end. A nurse might comfort a woman by telling her that her labor pains will be over "soon." They still hurt as much as they did before, perhaps to the point of seeming unbearable. But there is something about knowing that there is an end to one's pain that may make it more bearable. However, it is small comfort to anyone in pain to be told that things could be worse. Knowing that another person has suffered more than I or that I could be worse off does not lessen the pain of my real, present suffering. So what are we to make of this reminder to Smith that he is not yet as bad off as Job? Is God acting like an athletic coach: "Suck up the pain and carry on"? Perhaps, but I don't think that is a sufficient explanation.

Neither of these reminders—your pain will be but one point on the infinite time line of your life, and others have suffered more than you now suffer—will bring cessation or even lessening of the pain. So neither of them should be understood to mean "Joseph, you aren't really suffering." Nor does either seem merely an admonition for him to be brave and "push on through the pain," as some say. Rather, these responses put Smith's suffering into context, giving him a perspective from which to understand it: your suffering will be over in a relatively short time, and to be a human being is to suffer. Others—God names

Job but could have named himself—have suffered and will suffer more than you; that's part of the human condition. "Consider your suffering in comparison to the rest of your life and in comparison to the suffering of others," the Lord says (and he will explicitly compare Smith's suffering to his own in the part of the letters now canonized as Doctrine and Covenants 122:8). That comparison will not lessen Smith's suffering, but it can give him understanding. Much of this section is devoted to the idea that God will give his children divine, exalting knowledge, a theme that begins here.

The verses are also suggestive of another theme in the section: triumph over one's enemies and over the suffering of mortality doesn't require God's intercession or call for his vengeance. Rather, triumph calls for peace. The response to Joseph Smith's legitimate grievances is "Peace be unto thy soul" (v. 7). Exaltation is not a matter of overcoming or conquering others. As the divine suffering we see in Moses 7:28–29 and 32–37 shows, it isn't a matter of overcoming the possibility of pain. Exaltation is a matter of peace.

THERE IS A TIME APPOINTED TO EVERY MAN

The first response to Joseph Smith's complaint focuses on him and implicitly admonishes him to have peace in his soul rather than a desire for vengeance. Yet the second response, beginning in verse 11, focuses on Smith's enemies and sounds like a promise of vengeance: "They who do charge thee with transgression, their hope shall be blasted, and their prospects shall melt away as the hoar frost melteth before the burning rays of the rising sun." Whatever Smith's enemies hope to achieve by accusing him of sin, whatever they envision coming about as a result, they will fail. And it is not just their particular hopes that will be blasted. *Hope* is singular rather than plural: they will lose hope itself. For the often-insightful theologians of the medieval period, hope was a theological virtue whose ultimate object was God, and the loss of hope was gravely sinful, equivalent to rejecting God.[10] Perhaps the Lord has something similar in mind: Smith's enemies' hope is not in God; he is not the ultimate object of their particular, intermediary hopes for Smith's destruction. So in the end they will find themselves hopeless. Paul says, "If in this life only we have hope in Christ, we are of all men most miserable" (1 Corinthians 15:19). In contrast, verse 11 suggests that since those who oppose Joseph Smith have not put their hope in Christ, they will ultimately be miserable because they will be without hope at all.

> Since the hopes of those who attack Joseph Smith and the Saints are not in Christ, ultimately their hopes will be fruitless.

But the promise that prophesies the judgment on Smith's adversaries is more significant for what it says beyond vengeance: "God hath set his hand and seal to change the times and seasons" (v. 12). Perhaps the wording is intended to echo Daniel 2:20–21: "Blessed be the name of God for ever and ever: for wisdom and might are his: and he changeth the times and the seasons: he removeth kings, and setteth up kings: he giveth wisdom unto the wise, and knowledge to them that know understanding." If we make that connection, we see that the threats against the Saints remain under the control of God. He can change the circumstances as his wisdom dictates. At least as likely, however, is that the wording of Doctrine and Covenants 121:12 reflects 1 Thessalonians 5:1–2: "Of the times and the seasons, brethren, ye have no need

---

10. Perhaps the most obvious medieval theologians of the virtues are Augustine (354–430) and Thomas Aquinas (1225–1274).

that I write unto you. For yourselves know perfectly that the day of the Lord so cometh as a thief in the night." As used in 1 Thessalonians, "times and seasons" appears to be a hendiadys (two words expressing the same meaning) referring to the end time. If so, verse 12 of section 121 tells us that the Lord has determined to bring about the end of worldly time, which would mean also the end of threats against his people. But to say that is not to make threats against others.

It is noteworthy that the Lord twice says that the hopes of Smith's enemies will come to naught. In verse 11 he says their hope will be "blasted," and in verse 14 he says their hopes will be "cut off." The 1828 edition of Webster's *American Dictionary of the English Language* defines *blasted* as "affected by some cause that checks growth, injures, impairs, destroys, or renders abortive."[11] The *Oxford English Dictionary* gives "stricken by meteoric or supernatural agency" and "blighted" as definitions in use in the nineteenth century.[12] For all intents and purposes, here *blasted* and *cut off* mean the same thing: in contrast to the hope offered by God, the hope of those who persecute Smith will not only fail, it will be *caused* to fail. The enemies may believe they are in control of events, but it is God who is in control.

In the next thirteen verses, God lays out explicitly (and, I assume, hyperbolically) what will happen not only to Smith's but also to the Church's enemies: Their understanding will be blinded (see v. 12). The suffering they intend for others will come on them (see v. 13). They and their male posterity will be wiped from the face of the earth. *Male* posterity is specified in this curse, for verse 15 uses a slightly cleaned-up version of an insulting biblical phrase: "not one of them is left to stand by the wall."[13]

---

11. Noah Webster, ed., *An American Dictionary of the English Language* (New York: S. Converse, 1828), s.v. "blasted."

12. Oxford English Dictionary Online, s.v. "blasted, adj."

13. See, for example, 1 Samuel 25:22; 1 Kings 14:10, 21:21; 2 Kings 9:8. The

That curse is the one that first suggests to me clearly that we are to understand these threats as hyperbole. It is impossible that the same God who will not punish people for Adam's transgression (see Articles of Faith 1:2) will destroy the entire male posterity of a sinner for their father's sin.

The hyperbole continues in verse 16: people who undertake to fight against those whom God has anointed will be cursed: "Cursed are all those that shall lift up the heel against mine anointed." The phrase "lifted up the heel" echoes Psalm 41:9, which is also echoed in John 13:18, where Jesus uses it to refer to Judas, his betrayer. Both instances concern a former friend who has become a betrayer, suggesting that the enemies the Lord has in mind in this verse are those who were once friends of Joseph Smith or the Church and have now turned against them. If so, then rather than the prophets, as we might at first suppose, the anointed could be those who have been washed and anointed in the temple—in the twenty-first century, those who have received their endowment. We see more evidence for this interpretation in that those who swear falsely against God's servants—his children ("my little ones")—will be severed from the ordinances of the temple (see vv. 18–19). That also suggests that the enemies and "mine anointed" may both be those who have been washed and anointed in the temple.

Whatever we think about that question, though, the hyperbolic punishments and curses continue and increase in intensity: the enemies will fail economically, their descendants will have no right to the priesthood, and it would be better for them if they had been executed by drowning (see vv. 20–22)! The condemnation concludes with a warning and a final threat: "Wo unto all those that discomfort my people, and drive,

---

phrase, which refers to male urination, always occurs in the Bible as an insult to those to whom it refers.

and murder, and testify against them, saith the Lord of Hosts; a generation of vipers shall not escape the damnation of hell" (v. 23). *Discomfort* doesn't mean only "to make uncomfortable," as it might seem at first glance. Just as in scripture *comfort* means "to give strength to" more than "to alleviate distress," *discomfort* means "to deprive of courage or strength of mind; to discourage, dishearten, dismay" rather than "to make uncomfortable."[14] Perhaps also relevant is an earlier, sixteenth- and seventeenth-century meaning, "to defeat in battle." The Lord of Hosts, the Commander of the armies of heaven, threatens the damnation of hell on those who have warred against the children of God! This series of curses is enough to take away the reader's breath.

What are we to make of the frightening and seemingly vengeful jeremiad of verses 11 through 23? Given the revelation ten years earlier (1829) of Doctrine and Covenants 19:4–13—that "eternal punishment" doesn't mean "punishment that never ends," but "God's punishment"—the threat of damnation in hell seems not to be a threat of never-ending damnation. And given what Doctrine and Covenants 76 (1832) teaches, except for the sons of perdition (about whose fate we know nothing; see vv. 45–46), the damnation threatened is not a never-ending torment of hellfire, as some Christians believe. The Lord must be speaking hyperbolically, so that what he says might be "more express" (19:7) for the enemies threatening the young church and its prophet.

Since the Lord downplays the ultimate significance of Joseph Smith's suffering—"thine adversity and thine afflictions shall be but a small moment" (Doctrine and Covenants 121:7)—perhaps his hyperbole in verses 11 through 24 is also meant to match what ought to have been hyperbole in Smith's prayer. And perhaps the hyperbole is of some comfort to Smith, whose com-

---

14. Oxford English Dictionary Online, s.v. "discomfort, v."

plaint the Lord is responding to: let your soul be at peace; those who persecute you and your followers will receive what they have earned, and what they have earned is concomitant with what you have suffered. You feel that you have suffered unbearably; I will threaten them with unbearable punishments. But, in fact, your suffering will not last forever or be as bad as you presently feel—and that implies that neither will their punish-

> The curses pronounced in verses 11 through 23 seem to be the Lord saying things "more expressly" rather than literally.

ment be as bad as I am making it sound and that it will not last forever. The point is that the Lord knows his people's suffering and will strengthen them.

Indeed, how God will strengthen the Saints becomes the theme of the next verses and a transition to his promises. God sees and knows the works of those who discomfort the Church, and "there is a time appointed for every man, according as his works shall be" (v. 25). Everyone will get what is coming to them. Right now, neither the Saints nor their persecutors get what they deserve, but a time is coming—in just "a small moment" (v. 7)— when both will get their just deserts. That is why Smith should be at peace. Presumably, the time coming is the end time to which God referred in verse 12 when he began these verses of doom and which is referred to again in verse 32, the time of "the finishing and the end . . . when every man shall enter into his eternal presence and into his immortal rest."

A PROPHETIC PROMISE: KNOWLEDGE

In spite of the way the end time is often portrayed, especially in popular films and books, in Doctrine and Covenants 121 it is not so much a time of doom as a time of promise. Verse 25 is the hinge between doom and promise—by word count, almost exactly the midpoint of the section. The punishments of the persecutors, to come at the appointed time, have been told. Now the Prophet receives a revelation of the promise to the Saints: "God shall give unto you knowledge" (v. 26). The narrative voice is no longer that of the Lord, but of Joseph Smith speaking in his role as inspired prophet and referring to God in the third person.

Although not necessary to our understanding of the scriptural promise, the original context of verse 26 is moving and underscores the prophetic character of it and the verses that follow:

> We beseech of you, brethren, that you bear with those who do not feel themselves more worthy than yourselves, while we exhort one another to a [reformation?], with one and all, both old and young, teachers and taught, both high and low, rich and poor, bond and free, male and female. Let honesty and sobriety, and candor and solemnity, and virtue and pureness, and meekness and simplicity crown our heads in every place, and in fine become as little children, without malice, guile, or hypocrisy. And now, brethren, after your tribulations, if you do [these?] things and exercise fervent prayer and faith in the sight of God always, he shall give unto you knowledge by his Holy Spirit, yea, by the unspeakable gift of the Holy Ghost, that has not been revealed since the world was until now.[15]

---

15. Joseph Smith, "20 March Letter," 13; spelling, capitalization, and punctuation standardized.

In this context, the promise of knowledge is in sharp and democratic contrast to the warnings to the persecutors. Notice that the promise of verse 26 is not the opposite of the persecutors' punishments—economic prosperity instead of economic ruin, for example. Instead, it is orthogonal to the plane of those punishments: *knowledge* instead of economic ruin. This is not what most people would expect as recompense for their suffering. If I complain of my suffering, I expect my consolation for that pain to be a promise of at least some antidote and perhaps hopefully some compensating pleasure. In this case, though, Joseph Smith complains of his suffering and is told it will be short in God's reckoning and that things could be worse: "Thou art not yet as Job" (v. 10). Then with Smith as his prophetic mouthpiece, God promises the Saints knowledge rather than either temporal relief from the suffering that Smith and they are enduring or victory over those who persecute him and the Church.

Both here and in Psalm 46 knowledge comes from ceasing to worry, from trusting God in a time of persecution or attack. And what knowledge is promised? Knowledge given by the gift of the Holy Ghost "that has not been revealed since the world was until now" (Doctrine and Covenants 121:26). Knowledge "which our forefathers have awaited with anxious expectation"; things "held in reserve" that will give them glory (v. 27). "Nothing shall be withheld" is the promise (v. 28). Quoting Colossians 1:16, with its apparent reference to powers brought into being at Creation,[16] verse 29 tells us that not even those powers will be withheld from those "who have endured valiantly for the gospel of Jesus Christ." Then comes a list of representative things promised. Like the list of punishments earlier, this is a hyperbolic list, a list of things about which one might wonder, things theolog-

---

16. Eduard Lohse, *Colossians and Philemon: A Commentary on the Epistles to the Colossians and to Philemon* (Philadelphia: Fortress, 1971), 50–51.

ical and things astronomical, as well as things overlapping the theological and astronomical (as one would expect of a theology that ultimately doesn't divide the world into the temporal and the spiritual—see Doctrine and Covenants 29:34). But in the end, the hyperbole becomes real: everything "ordained in the midst of the Council of the Eternal God of all other gods before this world was" will be revealed, all the things ordained "for the finishing [of the world] and the end [in other words, purpose] thereof" (v. 32).

> In lieu of vengeance on their enemies, the knowledge that God promises his suffering Saints is that which comes through the Spirit. Ultimately it is the knowledge of all things.

Perhaps alluding to the waters of the nearby Missouri River, verse 33 summarizes the previous twenty-six verses with this unique metaphorical and rhetorical question: "How long can rolling waters remain impure?"[17] Presumably, the answer is "Not forever." But the metaphor is strange since rolling waters churn up silt and debris from the bottom, clouding water rather than clearing it. Perhaps it should be understood to mean something like "Even though the Missouri River's rolling waters are presently, and well known to be, muddy and unclear, how long can that go on? Not forever." Another rhetorical question in verse 33 repeats the point:

---

17. I recognize that in the original letter the phrase "rolling waters" refers to something other than the Missouri River (see Smith, "20 March Letter," 15). But our task is to understand the canonized text as it is for us in scripture today. The problems of some of its difficult passages may be insurmountable, in which case we must turn outside the text. But otherwise we will stick with the text as we have it. In the verses of section 121 as presently constituted, the connection between the rolling waters and the Missouri River is plausible.

"What power shall stay the heavens?" None. If the Missouri River cannot resist the power of God, then surely neither can the enemies of the Saints. The slightly changed metaphor repeats the point: what is the likelihood that those who oppose the Saints will be able to keep the Lord from "pouring down knowledge from heaven" on them? As likely as a man changing the course of or stopping the Missouri River by "stretch[ing] forth his puny arm" (v. 33). Nothing can stop God from doing what he will.

Sometimes we expect that valiant obedience will bring us economic or social prosperity. That is how we often think about what it means to prosper. But section 121 has a different notion of prosperity and its timing: those who are valiant are promised that they will prosper by receiving knowledge that brings glory (v. 27) and the powers of divine beings, and they will receive that knowledge at the end of time, when "God hath set his hand and seal to change the times and seasons" (v. 12). To prosper is to know that exaltation is promised in the end times and, therefore, to have hope—even in Liberty Jail. Since, as section 27 strongly suggests, the restoration of all things has begun, it makes sense to say that we are already in the end times. God has already begun to pour out divine knowledge "by the unspeakable gift of the Holy Ghost," knowledge "that has not been revealed since the world was until now" (121:26). But, as the metaphor of verse 45b will suggest, it may not be immediately obvious to us that we are receiving it.

> The Saints are also promised prosperity, but prosperity seems to mean hope for divine knowledge and glory more than it means economic or social prosperity.

By the time we get to verse 36, section 121 has taken us from Joseph Smith's complaint against God to God's admonition of soulful peace, followed by promises that when all is said and done everyone will receive either the condemnation they have earned or the gift of knowledge with which God blesses his people. It would be possible for this revelation to end there. The Lord has answered Joseph Smith's complaint and his demand for revenge with his blessing and these promises. But it continues with a rebuke and more promises.

THE CALLED AND THE CHOSEN: THE POWERS OF HEAVEN

As the *we* of verse 37 shows, we hear the same narrative voice in verse 34 that began in verse 26, the voice of the Prophet Joseph Smith. But we see a sudden shift in theme. The canonized section has so far taken the form of a prophetic dialogue: Joseph Smith praying for relief and vengeance, God responding to him with peace, then through Smith a promise of knowledge. In verse 34 Smith's prophecy continues. But whereas to this point power has been an implicit question—Will the Lord exercise it? How will he? What power is promised the Saints?—now the topic becomes explicit: people are not chosen, though called, because they do not use the powers of heaven properly.

As I read this, Joseph Smith has been explicitly comforted and implicitly rebuked by the conversation with the Lord that we have seen in the first 33 verses, especially by the admonition to be at peace and the reminder that he has friends, perhaps as well by the Lord's condemnations of the persecutors. Now, speaking prophetically, Smith shares what he has learned: "there are many called" to receive the knowledge that God has promised, "but few are chosen" to actually receive it (v. 34). Why do only a few receive it? For two reasons: First, because "their hearts are set so much upon the things of this world." In particular, they "aspire to the honors of men" (v. 35). The second reason follows from the first: they are not chosen because they do not learn how priesthood rights can be used (see v. 36). The first applies broadly, but perhaps especially to those who have vilified Joseph Smith and persecuted the Saints. They desire the praise of men rather than the knowledge of God. Perhaps the second is a particular rebuke to Smith: he has not understood that heaven's power cannot be controlled by the desire for vengeance.

But if the previous discussion of knowledge has been a rebuke to Joseph Smith, it has a been a mild one. Now, in Smith's own narrative voice, we will hear something more direct: "No power or influence can or ought to be maintained by virtue of the priesthood, only by persuasion, by long-suffering, by gentleness and meekness, and by love unfeigned" (v. 41). If Smith's prayer at the beginning of the section is a prayer for vengeance, for compulsion and power obtained by force, then verses 34 through 41 are a rebuke of him, though still indirectly.

However, regardless of how one understands these verses in relationship to Joseph Smith, they rebuke readers today: "We have learned by sad experience that it is the nature and disposition of *almost all men*, as soon as they get a little authority, as they suppose, they will immediately begin to exercise unrighteous dominion" (v. 39; emphasis added). Almost all of us naturally use our authority—the power of some kind that we have over other beings—unrighteously, presumably in the ways described in verse 37. The rights of the priesthood are poured out on many in the temple and given to many through ordination and settings apart. Many are called. And those priesthood rights are "inseparably connected with the powers of heaven" (v. 36): they can be used only on principles of righteousness. Only those who use them in that way are chosen.

Of course, righteousness is a matter of moral purity, one of the things participants in the temple rite covenant to abide by; but righteousness is not *only* moral purity, nor is it the only object of their covenants. In fact, righteousness is not mostly moral purity. In the Old Testament, when referring to God, the word translated "righteousness" is usually used to speak of what he does to save his people. For example, Psalm 98:2–3 says: "The Lord hath made known his salvation: his righteousness hath he openly shewed in the sight of the heathen. He hath remembered his mercy [*ḥesed*: "loving kindness"] and his truth [*'ĕmûnâ*: "fidelity"] toward the house of Israel: all the ends of the earth have seen the salvation of our God." Similarly, Psalm 119:40–41 says: "Behold, I have longed after thy precepts: quicken me [give me life] in thy righteousness. Let thy mercies come also unto me, O Lord, even thy salvation, according to thy word." When referring to human beings, the meaning of *righteousness* is usually "right action," but we must not forget that what it means for a human being to act rightly ought to be modeled on what it means for the Lord to act righteously. Just as divine righteousness is most often connected with salvation and mercy, so should our own righteousness take them as its end.

In the Hebrew Bible the word translated "righteous" (*ṣaddîq*) can mean the proper order of life and, so, right conduct before God in all of its facets, including our sexual behavior. We see that meaning especially in the psalms. But human righteousness in keeping the law is an imitation of the Lord's righteousness, which is to restore proper order to human society when it has become disordered. Human relations can be disordered in many ways,

> Righteousness is not only moral rectitude. It is a matter of working as God's agent in offering salvation and mercy to our fellows in the many ways that is possible.

sexual sin among them. But the Hebrew Bible more often understands the disorder of our relations as the abuse of the widow, the fatherless, or the stranger[18]—doing injustice to the disadvantaged—and as King Benjamin makes clear, the person who is in a right relationship with God will be the agent for healing that disorder (see Mosiah 4:11, 16–23). Such people will act as if in God's saving stead in their relationships. That is the fundamental principle of righteousness.

Perhaps that is the essence of the priesthood powers and why they are inseparably connected with the powers of heaven: priesthood power is the power to bless others in the name of God. We see it in such things as blessings for the sick and in what leaders do to administer the Church, but we also see it in the work of the Primary teachers who have been called by God to bless the children in their class and the work of ministers called to bless the lives of their fellow congregants. In all such positions we have the right to divine knowledge through the Holy Ghost. That is the power of heaven that makes it possible for a person to exercise the rights of the priesthood on principles of righteousness. That is the knowledge planned for in the Council in Heaven and awaited by our ancestors.

I think this is the doctrine of the priesthood: nothing will be withheld *unless* we do not use the priesthood power we have been blessed with to bless the lives of others, in other words, unless we do not use it righteously as guided by the Holy Ghost. If we try to hide our sins from God, to gratify our pride or vain ambition, or to exercise unrighteous dominion or compulsion over others *in any degree*, then "amen" to the knowledge that has been promised (see Doctrine and Covenants 121:37). The Holy Spirit will withdraw, grieved by our offense, and we will be left

---

18. For a good overview of the Hebrew Bible's understanding of righteousness, see John J. Scullion, "Righteousness: Old Testament," in *The Anchor Yale Bible Dictionary*, ed. David Noel Freedman (New York: Doubleday, 1992), 5:724–36.

to ourselves. We will have nothing but our own resources to rely on. We will be without the divine knowledge that can make us like the gods. We will be bereft of the knowledge we need for the finishing and purposes of the world (see v. 32).

Unfortunately, though, experience teaches that almost any persons, given what they suppose is some degree of authority, will immediately begin to use that authority for purposes other than to bless others (see v. 39). They may use it to make themselves seem better than they are, to satisfy their need for self-pride, to satisfy their ambition to get ahead of others, or to control or compel others. But we have been told what the outcome of that behavior will be: the loss of the promised blessing of knowledge and, so, of exaltation. Thus, as the revelation repeats to end the inclusio

> I understand the doctrine of the priesthood to be that without the guidance of the Holy Ghost we will be unable to do the Father's will "on earth as it is [done] in heaven" (3 Nephi 13:10).

that began in verse 34, "many are called" to receive God's knowledge, "but few are chosen" to actually have it (v. 40).

On my reading, Doctrine and Covenants 121 teaches a frightening doctrine, something that, in his suffering, Joseph Smith had learned through his encounter with God: many of us are called to receive the blessing of membership and of the endowment, the gift of divine knowledge through the Holy Ghost. Instead, having our hearts set on the things of this world and being honored by others, most of us refuse to receive what has been poured out on us—though that refusal is rarely conscious; we do it naturally, without having to think about it. As a result, in spite of having been called, most of us are not among the chosen. We do not yet receive the divine knowledge promised, and "it is impossible for a [person] to be saved in ignorance" (131:6). It seems like our situation is dire.

PERSUASION, REPROOF, AND THE PROMISE OF CONFIDENCE BEFORE GOD

But section 121 does not end with the frightening thought that comes from the rebuke in verses 34 through 40, offered to us in a timely and pointed manner. The section goes on to instruct us in how to receive the promised knowledge, now in what seems to be the narrative voice of the Lord rather than the Prophet. In contrast with the human drive for power over others, we can receive the knowledge promised by exercising whatever power we have been given in the seeming weakness of the way of Jesus Christ, namely "by persuasion, by long-suffering, by gentleness and meekness, and by love unfeigned; by kindness and pure knowledge, which shall greatly enlarge the soul [that is] without hypocrisy and without guile" (vv. 41–42; punctuation modified).

Presumably this requires our intentionality. As verse 39 implies, these ways of behaving do not come naturally to most of us. But we can hew to the divine model of Jesus Christ. That model, described in verses 41 and 42, tells us how we have power, though "power" in this case does not mean "power over another." It means, instead, "the ability to do the work of God, the power to do what makes our souls greater." We can have the power to do the work of God if we will live seemingly weak lives of gentleness, meekness, love, kindness, and pure knowledge rather than lives of domination.

Most of the things listed in verses 41 and 42 are self-explanatory, except perhaps "pure knowledge." Its most obvious meaning is something like "knowledge that is untainted with falsehood." But we might also take it to mean "knowledge of things that are pure." That is, presumably, the knowledge already promised in verses 26 and 33 and described in the verses between—namely, the promised knowledge of the gods.

If, after using gentleness, meekness, and unfeigned love to influence others, reproof is needed, it should be given early (the meaning of the word *betimes*) and with sharpness (v. 43). But does *sharpness* mean "severity" or does it mean "acuity"? I believe that the second meaning fits the context better than the first. We sometimes read verse 43 to mean "occasionally reproving severely, when the Holy Ghost tells us to," but I believe it means "reproving early with acuity, when the Holy Ghost moves us to." Reproof, too, must be gentle, meek, and a demonstration of unfeigned love—*as God's response has been to Joseph Smith's complaint*. And even if it is all of that, it is essential that we show more love to the person we have reproved so that he or she doesn't think we are an enemy, someone trying to cause damage or evil to them. Our love must be such that our faithfulness—our loyalty—to the person is "stronger than the cords of death" (v. 44).

The image of the cords of death is striking, even frightening. Though the King James translation of Psalm 18:4 speaks of "the sorrows [*hebel*] of death," other translations of the same verse (e.g., the New International Version) read "the

> If reproof is needed, it should be early and accurate—and meted out with love stronger than death itself.

cords of death." Places in the Hebrew Bible use similar language. For example, 2 Samuel 22:6 refers to "the snares of death" using *hebel*; Job 36:8 speaks of "cords of affliction"; Isaiah 5:18 warns of being drawn by "cords of vanity" or falsehood. In a more obviously similar way, Abinadi refers to "the bands of death" (Mosiah 15:8). In each case the cords or bands are something difficult or impossible to break free from, a trap or a snare. The point of the image in Psalm 18:4 and Mosiah 15:8 is that we cannot break free from death. Nothing is more final nor, it would seem, more everlasting. But the revelation of section 121 turns what is otherwise a frightening image, an image only attenuated by the hope for resurrection, into a metaphor for love: our faithfulness to our sister or brother must be even stronger than the seemingly unbreakable bands of death. That is what it looks like to have received the knowledge of God, the ability to act in our relationships with others as we see him acting in his relationships with us, in a faithfulness that is stronger than death, indeed so strong that it has overcome death in order to rescue us. Like that love, our faithfulness to those with whom we are in relation must go through and beyond even death.

The first half of verse 45 follows by summarizing how we are to use priesthood power: "Let thy bowels also be full of charity towards all men," reminding us indirectly of Joseph Smith's plea in verse 4 that the Lord's bowels would be "moved with compassion toward [the Saints]"—and perhaps mildly chastising him for his lack of charity in that prayer, as understandable as that lack might be. (His prayer is especially understandable in light of the addition to the command to be charitable that reminds us of our particular duty to be charitable "to the household of faith." Smith was concerned not only for his own situation but for the Saints in general, a concern that we see in the first six verses of the section.)

Besides having charity, we are to "let virtue garnish [our] thoughts unceasingly." Like righteousness, in scripture *virtue* means more than chastity; it means excellence.[19] *Garnish* is not a word we use much except when we are referring to things with which we might decorate a plate of food, such as a parsley sprig,

---

19. Webster, *American Dictionary of the English Language*, s.v. "virtue."

or alternatively and strangely when we speak of a legal claim against a person's wages. But neither of those meanings makes sense here. It makes no sense to speak of decorating my thoughts with excellence; excellence ought to be more than merely a decoration. Nor can we use the legal sense of *garnish* in this verse, "to seize part of someone's income in payment of a debt." But there is an older meaning that fits: "to furnish" or "to supply."[20] *Garnish* also means to beautify, to clothe in elegance.[21] The commandment is to supply our thoughts with excellence, or to improve and grace them with virtue rather than with superficial adornment.

In contrast to the ways almost all of us act when we think we have been given a little authority (see vv. 35–39), verses 41 through 45a tell us that authority can be used only in charity, and they give concrete examples of what that means: persuasion rather than command, patience rather than frustration, meekness rather than pride, genuine love rather than pretended care, kindness rather than harshness, and pure knowledge rather than merely the knowledge of the world.

FINAL PROMISES: EVERLASTING DOMINION

The second half of verse 45 and all of verse 46 introduce the final set of four promises leading to their culmination in a fifth:

1. "Then shall thy confidence wax strong in the presence of God."
2. "The doctrine of the priesthood shall distil upon thy soul as the dews from heaven."
3. "The Holy Ghost shall be thy constant companion."

---

20. Webster, *American Dictionary of the English Language*, s.v. "garnish."
21. Oxford English Dictionary Online, s.v. "garnish, v."

4. "Thy scepter [shall be] an unchanging scepter of righteousness and truth."
5. "Thy dominion shall be an everlasting dominion, and without compulsory means it shall flow unto thee forever and ever."

The first of these may be a response to Joseph's initial prayer: "If you learn to exercise the powers of the priesthood as I teach you here to do, you will be confident before me rather than fearful before men and pitiable before me." But for those reading verse 45 today, this is also an astounding promise: do the things taught in verses 41 through 45a and you will be confident before God: you will be able to stand before him without fear or shame; you will be exalted.

What would make us lack confidence before him? First of all, sin. Like 1 Peter 4:8, Doctrine and Covenants 121:45 teaches in different words that "charity shall cover the multitude of sins." The traditional text of the verse in 1 Peter has something to teach us: the Greek word for "cover" is *kaluptō*, "to cover or hide something," "to make something secret." It is one of the roots of the word *apocalypse*, meaning literally "the uncovering." King Benjamin agrees, teaching that lives of genuine charity will secure the remission of sins that we gain by repentance (see Mosiah 4:20–23): charity will make our previously sinful life remain under erasure, remitted, covered over.

It does not follow that charity but not moral purity is required, though much of Jesus's preaching in the New Testament is directed against those who confuse righteousness with legalistic moral purity, with mere obedience to the law. As he says in Matthew 23:23: "Woe unto you, scribes and Pharisees, hypocrites! for ye pay tithe of mint and anise and cummin, and have omitted the weightier matters of the law, judgment, mercy, and faith: these ought ye to have done, *and not to leave the other undone*" (emphasis added). Judgment, mercy, and faith, and we can add charity, are even weightier matters than moral purity, though they are less easy for us to judge, especially in others. But it is not a matter of one or the other. Neither is to be left undone.

We also learn something by looking at 1 Peter 4:8 as Joseph Smith revised it: "Charity *preventeth* a multitude of sins."[22] Sins are offenses against others of some kind or another, even when we think they are something that concerns ourselves alone. John Donne's (1572–1631) "Meditation XVII" has become almost a cliché.[23] In spite of that, it says something directly applicable to this question when it begins "No man is an island entire of itself" and ends by reminding us that we should "never send to know for whom / the bell tolls; it tolls for thee." Donne reminds us that "any man's death diminishes me, / because I am involved in mankind." What is true of death is also true of sin since the latter is a type of the former: another person falling into sin diminishes me because I am part of the human web that includes that other person. Likewise, my fall into sin diminishes all of humanity. Any person's diminishment as a human being diminishes us all; there is no private or victimless sin. Our love for others is incomplete when we fall into sin, so complete charity would prevent sin. The promise of section 121 is that the charity that imitates God's love for all will overcome sin and make us confident before him.

Besides sin, an obvious reason that we might not have confidence before God is that we recognize our weakness as finite human beings. It isn't just that we sin, but that we are fallible and humanly weak. Doesn't King Benjamin tell us that we must recognize that weakness if we are to retain a remission of our sins (see Mosiah 4:11), and doesn't recognizing our finitude preclude confidence before the majesty of Almighty God? How can

---

22. "Joseph Smith Translation," https://www.churchofjesuschrist.org/study/scriptures/jst/jst-1-pet/4; emphasis added.

23. John Donne, "Meditation XVII," *Devotions upon Emergent Occasions*, http://www.luminarium.org/sevenlit/donne/meditation17.php.

a person both recognize her weakness and be confident? There is a contradiction between the two only if our confidence is *self-confidence*. If we receive a remission of our sins and recognize our weakness before God and his great power, we can be confident in his power rather than ours. If we recognize our weakness and his almighty power, then when we act as he does, with charity for all, we can trust in his power to bring about what he will. Whatever our reason for not having confidence before God might be, it will be overcome by charity.

Doctrine and Covenants 121 concludes by making a series of promises of what will come to us if we live lives of charity and excellence. The first, and perhaps the most difficult to understand, is that "the doctrine of the priesthood shall distil upon [our] soul[s] as the dews from heaven" (v. 45). Section 121 has earlier told us that the hope of those who persecute the Saints will melt away with the morning sun—the sun of the days to come with the Restoration—like the light frost that coats everything on a winter night (v. 11). But for the Saints, the same phenomenon, the condensation of moisture caused by cool night air, is the metaphor for a blessing that comes naturally and perhaps unnoticed on a late spring morning: the teaching of the priesthood will settle on us all but imperceptibly until we awake in the morning to see the way it has transformed and cleansed our perception, making everything new again.

> Confidence before God isn't self-confidence—it is confidence in him and his promises, and faith in his power rather than our own.

But what is the doctrine of the priesthood? In the context of this revelation, it seems to me to refer to the knowledge promised in verses 26 through 32, the knowledge that God pours down "upon the heads of the Latter-day Saints" (v. 33)—indeed, that he pours down through the Prophet in those very verses. This is knowledge in which "nothing [is] withheld" (v. 28), knowledge "ordained in the midst of the Council of the Eternal God of all other gods before this world was" (v. 32). It was anxiously anticipated by our forebears (v. 27) and is the knowledge given "by the unspeakable gift of the Holy Ghost" (v. 26) and repeated in verse 46, the constant companionship of the Holy Ghost. The last of these is perhaps key to them all: the doctrine of the priesthood is whatever is revealed by the Holy Spirit, and through him comes the promise that nothing will be withheld from those whose "bowels [are] full of charity towards all" and who unceasingly give sustenance to their thoughts with the things that are best (v. 45).

If we live the virtuous and charitable lives described in verses 41 through 45a, the revelations of the Holy Ghost will come to us like dew quietly forming on blades of grass. Then the commandment given at our confirmation—"Receive the Holy Ghost"—will be fulfilled, for the Holy Ghost will be our constant companion (v. 46) and "nothing shall be withheld" from us (v. 28). Then we will have the dominion of God, everlasting dominion, as our own. Then "all that [the] Father hath shall be given unto [us]" (84:38).

As Alma taught at the waters of Mormon, the desire to live charitably prepares us to receive the covenant of baptism (see Mosiah 18:8–9). We see here that the ordinance of confirmation, with its command to receive the Holy Ghost, points us toward the fulfilment of that confirmation, that "making fast,"[24] in "charity towards all men, and to the household of faith" (v. 45). Charity in the beginning; charity in the end.

---

24. See the etymology: Oxford English Dictionary Online, s.v. "confirm, v."

CONCLUSION

The beginning of Doctrine and Covenants 121, Joseph Smith's complaint at his powerlessness against the enemies of the Church and his imprisonment (verses 1–6), is answered at the end of the section with a promise of power and a kingdom (see v. 46). But that answer to Smith's complaint is not a promise of power over his enemies. Instead, it is a promise of a dominion in which any authority that he has is made visible in the scepter of his righteousness and truth. In European and some other kingdoms, scepters were ceremonial staffs representing the king's authority. They were a physical symbol of that which held him up as king, of his power. The promise to those whose bowels are full of charity is that they will receive the doctrine of the priesthood gently, like the dew of heaven, and that they will be held up by righteousness and truth. As we have seen, the power held up by righteousness and truth is the inverse of the power of the world. Rather than power over others, which causes the Spirit to withdraw, it is the inverse of worldly power. It is what often appears to be weakness in the eyes of the world: love and excellence—and the power of righteousness and truth brings the Spirit in fullness. Rather than the temporary power over others that vengeance and compulsion could bring but that can never be more than temporary, Joseph Smith and we are promised everlasting dominions, in other words, dominions given by He Who Is Everlasting.

> We are promised eternal dominions undergirded by righteousness and truth if the Holy Ghost is our constant companion and the scepter of our rule is righteousness and truth.

The phrase "righteousness and truth" occurs in only one other place in scripture, in the King James translation of Ephesians 5:8–9: "Now are ye light in the Lord: walk as children of light: (for the fruit of the Spirit is in all goodness and righteousness and truth)." The parallel of the phrase's use in those verses with its use in verse 46 is striking. Paul admonishes the Ephesians to live as children of light because of the light they have received in the Lord, which they can do because the fruit of the Spirit is in everything that is good, righteous, and true. That sounds very much like the admonition of this section: live in the goodness, truth, and righteousness received from the Lord, which is possible because he has given us the Holy Spirit.

As the last verses of Doctrine and Covenants 121 make clear, this is a revelation of how we are to be related to others: through persuasion, long-suffering, gentleness, and meekness; by kindness and the soul-enlarging knowledge of pure things given by the Holy Ghost—all things that take us to "love unfeigned" (v. 41). But it is also a rebuke, perhaps to Joseph Smith, but certainly to those who, having received the divine gift of the Holy Ghost and of the endowment, then use those gifts for anything other than to bless the lives of God's other children by working in righteousness and truth to heal the disorders that affect them, whether physical, mental, personal, familial, or societal.

> Only the knowledge that comes to those whose love is genuine and who use the gifts of the priesthood to bless others can receive "an everlasting dominion" that flows to a person "without compulsory means . . . forever and ever."

Exergue

Properly speaking, scripture should have the last word. It is presumptuous of me to add anything afterward, like deciding to make myself the final speaker in church, inserting myself into the program after the bishop has spoken. But many will find this book and its argument sufficiently strange that I need to add something, like an inscription on a coin that neither adds to nor detracts from its value, but may help give it a place in our currency.

The first point of this book is that perhaps when we Latter-day Saints have done theology we have not been as attentive to the revelations of Joseph Smith as we ought to have been. I believe that we have often unknowingly continued to use as background assumptions beliefs about God that are incompatible with what Joseph Smith taught. In particular, we have assumed that there must ultimately be something corresponding at least roughly to Parmenides's understanding of the ultimate basis of reality—namely, an unchanging metaphysical entity that many ancients called "the One" and that traditional Christianity inherited for much of its thinking about God and divine things.

But that explains only the first three chapters. The most obvious question a reader might have after reading those chapters is what the initial discussion of the One and the Many has to do with the theory of scripture in chapter 4 and the interpretations of scripture in chapters 5 and 6. Of course, I hope that readers have seen the connection as they went along, but sometimes even when you see something as it happens, you're not sure what you saw when it is all over. The parts don't add up to a whole for you.

When we see the world through the prism of the atemporal, unchanging metaphysical One, we look for a final meaning of any particular thing and of the world as a whole. That might be the original meaning, what the prophet was thinking when he wrote the words we are reading. It might be the objective truth discoverable using the tools of the historian. Or it might be, instead, the meaning toward which we will all eventually be led, the meaning we will all agree on in the end. The Western philosophical tradition has explained truth in a variety of ways. But if what-is is eternally multiple rather than singular, if there is eternally more than one kind of thing in existence, as Joseph Smith has revealed, and if those things can continue to be in changing relationships (e.g., relationships of growth), then things, events, and texts can have any number of meanings, though never just whatever meaning we wish to impute to them.

If we understand the gospel to be about relationships rather than about objects of some kind—our relationships with the Godhead, with our divine Parents, and with each other—there *is* a sense in which there is ultimately only one thing: the relationship of love. But as a relationship rather than an object, that one thing is never the same except for its constancy. It continues. As a relationship, love is always a matter of more than one and, so, never a matter of the Parmenidean One.

I have loved my wife for almost fifty years, and our love has been constant. But it hasn't always meant the same thing, nor does it seem headed toward some ultimate, final meaning. It was one thing for an engaged couple eager to be married, another for a young married couple with babies in the house, yet another as a couple in our forties dealing with teenagers, and it has become something else entirely as we have become grandparents and foresee great-grandchildren in the not-so-distant future. Our love doesn't just change from epoch to epoch of our lives; it changes from week to week and day to day. The constancy of our love, our faithfulness to each other and to our relationship, has had many meanings and continues to have still more. Nothing in our experience suggests that we will reach a point where we will say, "Now we are done with that. Now we are finished with the truth of love." To reach such a point would be to have reached the end of our relationship. Yet, at the same time, we can honestly say that we love each other fully and have done so for many years. I have argued that knowing divine truth is probably more like that than it is like the static truths of geometry or physics (which appear to perhaps not be as static as was once thought).

Our study of the revelations of God, through both ancient and modern prophets, ought to enact our relationship to his love for us and the need that we have to love him and our neighbor. Yet the enactment of his constant love and our need for constancy in love is never said in just one way, nor is there ever an end of saying it. How God's love is enacted changes as our relationships change, not because we see things differently (though we do) but because we live in the world differently if we see what the prophets reveal. But those changes in how divine love is enacted do not mean that God did not love us fully before the changes. In fact, they mean the opposite: the changes in how his love is enacted are evidence that his love for us is full.

Our study of what God has revealed continues because his love continues. He is not a thing, like a rock or distant galaxy. He is a person. So he is not to be understood by understanding his properties so much as by understanding his relationships with his children. Presumably, his divine properties will be visible in those relationships, but in order to know him it is not enough to know them. He gives us the scriptures as a sign of his relationships, but like any sign, their meaning depends not only on what the person who received the sign and posted it for us intended it to mean, but on the context into which it has been put. We must be attentive to the particulars of the signs he has given in order to know what they mean for us in their present context—a context that is rarely that of just some small moment in time. The context of the scriptures may be constantly changing as the world changes, but it always includes the distant past and the promised future.

As I read Moses 5:1–12, it shows us the necessity of prayer, obedience, and sacrifice; it reflects on the positive consequences of Adam and Eve's transgression; and it urges us to repent. In the process of doing so, it teaches us the necessity of living in this real world rather than in some idyllic ideal world. We must live in a world where the fullness of life requires labor and pain, but we also live in a world in which covenant mercy can give meaning to our lives together and promise to our lives hereafter.

Similarly, as I read Doctrine and Covenants 121, it teaches us that real power is the power to be like God, which means ultimately the power to love and serve others rather than to have vengeance for our suffering. Real power comes quietly, perhaps unnoticed, as we live lives of charity and receive the teaching of the priesthood and the companionship of the Holy Ghost. Real power means charity that imitates the charity of Christ.

But what I say here does not summarize *the* meaning of the passages. I believe that I've described possible and reasonable meanings (plural). But we could collect a dozen different readings of the same verses by other readers, and all of them might make sense and be profitable to us, even if it is not possible to bring them all together in one larger whole—except the whole of the ongoing love of God. The depths of God's love and the multiplicity of those he loves in the manifold of their lives make a legion of meanings possible, even necessary. The theology enacted in scripture is a theology of the manifold in relation to God rather than a theology of the One.

Recommendations for Further Reading

For those interested in reading more on the history of philosophy and theology, here are a few suggestions.

1. Those looking for a brief overview of a particular thinker will be best served by the podcasts *History of Philosophy without Any Gaps*, https://historyofphilosophy.net/. These are short lectures on major thinkers in the history of philosophy, more than one for the most important thinkers, like Plato and Aristotle. These are excellent.

2. For online articles concerning particular individual topics or figures, the Stanford Encyclopedia of Philosophy is also an excellent resource: https://plato.stanford.edu/.

3. Among print works, perhaps the best detailed history of Western philosophy is the eight-volume work of Frederick C. Copleston, SJ: *A History of Philosophy* (Image Books). These were first published in the 1960s but have not gone out of print. The series is old but remains a classic.

4. Apart from that eight-volume series, Copleston has also written an excellent overview of medieval philosophy: *A History of Medieval Philosophy* (Harper Torchbooks, 1972), 346 pages.

5. Routledge published a ten-volume series in 2003 that is first-rate, each volume written by a specialist of the period or topic. For a listing, see https://www.routledge.com/Routledge -History-of-Philosophy/book-series/SE0159:

> C. C. W Taylor, *From the Beginning to Plato*, 528 pages
> David Furley, *From Aristotle to Augustine*, 480 pages
> John Marenbon, *Medieval Philosophy*, 548 pages
> G. H. R. Parkinson, *The Renaissance and 17th Century Rationalism*, 480 pages
> Stuart Brown, *British Philosophy and the Age of Enlightenment*, 440 pages
> Kathleen Higgins and Robert C. Solomon, *The Age of German Idealism*, 448 pages
> C. L. Ten, *The Nineteenth Century*, 496 pages
> Richard Kearney, *Continental Philosophy of the 20th Century*, 576 pages
> Stuart G. Shanker, *Philosophy of Science, Logic and Mathematics in the 20th Century*, 504 pages
> John V. Canfield, *Philosophy of Meaning, Knowledge and Value in the Twentieth Century*, 504 pages

6. In the late 1980s and the early 1990s, Oxford University Press began a similar series, A History of Western Philosophy, each by a specialist. Eight books were projected, seven of which have been completed:

> Terence Irwin, *Classical Thought* (1989), 249 pages
> David Luscombe, *Medieval Thought* (1997), 242 pages
> Brian P. Copenhaver and Charles B. Schmitt, *Renaissance Philosophy* (1992), 357 pages
> John Cottingham, *The Rationalists* (1988), 225 pages
> R. S. Woolhouse, *The Empiricists* (1988), 161 pages

Robert C. Solomon, *Continental Philosophy since 1750:*
The Rise and Fall of the Self (1988), 202 pages
John Skorupski, *English-Language Philosophy, 1750–1945*
(1993), 202 pages

Each of these is very good. I especially like Solomon's contribution. Volume 8, Barry Stroud, *English Language Philosophy since 1945*, appears not to have been published.

7. Anthony Kenny has written a one-volume comprehensive history: *A New History of Western Philosophy* (Oxford, 2010), 1058 pages. Kenny's book is strong through modern philosophy (up to about 1800) and strong on Anglo-American philosophy thereafter. His account of Continental European philosophy in the nineteenth and twentieth centuries is weaker.

8. Another one-volume history, *The Columbia History of Western Philosophy*, edited by Richard H. Popkin (Columbia, 1999), 864 pages, is written by a collection of scholars rather than by one person and, as a result, has the advantage of expertise on each figure or topic discussed.

9. Julián Marías's survey of Western philosophy is also excellent: *History of Philosophy* (Dover, 1967), 545 pages. Like Copleston's series, Marías's book is slightly old-fashioned. But its coverage is complete, and his understanding of the history of philosophy is strong, with clear explanations of difficult ideas.

10. For a shorter (though still not short) overview with a more contemporary approach (and written in an American idiom), consider Robert C. Solomon and Kathleen M. Higgins, *A Short History of Philosophy* (Oxford, 1996), 313 pages.

11. Finally, Rémi Brague has written four books that, though not histories of philosophy in the strict sense, are relevant to the issues of this book. Three of them are philosophical histories of an idea:

The Wisdom of the World: The Human Experience of the Universe in Western Thought (Chicago, 2003), 265 pages
The Law of God: The Philosophical History of an Idea (Chicago, 2007), 320 pages
The Kingdom of Man: Genesis and Failure of the Modern Project (Notre Dame, 2018), 267 pages

Each of these is interesting not only for the way it sheds light on a particular idea or movement in Western thought, but also for the way the history of that idea sheds light more broadly on Western history and culture as a whole.

Brague's fourth book is on medieval philosophy and theology: *The Legend of the Middle Ages: Philosophical Explorations of Medieval Christianity, Judaism, and Islam* (Chicago, 2009), 278 pages. All four of these are highly readable and generally accessible.

Index

About the Author

James E. Faulconer is a Senior Research Fellow at the Neal A. Maxwell Institute for Religious Scholarship. He has a PhD in philosophy from The Pennsylvania State University. He is married to Janice K. Allen, and they have four children and thirteen grandchildren. Faulconer has published in philosophy and psychology as well as in Latter-day Saint theology. He is the author of the Made Harder series, questions for Latter-day Saint scripture study.